LAND USE AND THE LEGISLATURES
The Politics of State Innovation

by

Nelson Rosenbaum

THE URBAN INSTITUTE is a nonprofit research organization established in 1968 to study problems of the nation's urban communities. Independent and nonpartisan, the Institute responds to current needs for disinterested analyses and basic information and attempts to facilitate the application of this knowledge. As a part of this effort, it cooperates with federal agencies, states, cities, associations of public officials, and other organizations committed to the public interest.

The Institute's research findings and a broad range of interpretive viewpoints are published as an educational service. The research and studies forming the basis for this publication were supported by a grant from the Ford Foundation. The work was undertaken in The Urban Institute's Land Use Center.

The interpretations or conclusions are those of the author and should not be attributed to The Urban Institute, its trustees, the Ford Foundation, or other organizations that support its research.

"It is one of the happy incidents of the
the federal system that a single courageous
state may, if its citizens choose, serve as
a laboratory and try novel social and economic
experiments without risk to the rest of the country."

Justice Louis D. Brandeis

Contents

List of Tables

Tables

Figure

Foreword

After decades of neglect, the states are being rediscovered as vital and powerful forces in urban governance. A widespread interest in the potential contribution of state government to better use of the nation's land resources has led to many pioneering statutes which place state agencies at the center of sensitive land use policy decisions.

In the last five years, numerous studies have appeared describing the ways in which the states are carving out a new role for themselves in planning and managing the use of land. While these studies have been useful in acquainting the public with what the leading states are trying to do, generally they have not examined state experience in a way which permits some conclusions to be drawn about the likely future spread of innovative laws to the other sister states. Such an understanding is vital to any assessment of how well our governments are responding to a set of commonly perceived problems. In particular, such an assessment is necessary to determine the scope and direction of national legislation aimed at spurring the states to reform land use practices within their borders.

This research is intended to fill this need. Utilizing a general framework of analysis derived from prior research on state legislative behavior, the study analyzes and predicts the spread of three different types of land use legislation: mandatory local growth management, major facility siting, and critical areas protection.

The author shows that the adoption of innovative land use statutes displays a marked regional pattern. Mandatory local planning, zoning, and subdivision control statutes, for example, have been adopted primarily in the western states while wetlands protection and large-scale development siting acts are concentrated largely in the northeast. The author attributes this regionalism to a number of factors, including intensive communications links between neighboring states, shared physical and social conditions, and common traditions of political culture. Only a few statutes demonstrate a "national" pattern of diffusion—rapid adoption among states in all regions of the nation. The author presents a detailed analysis of the conditions which lead to the "nationalization" of an innovation.

A constant theme within the study is the interplay of federal initiative and state response. The analysis shows that the federal government has played a vital role in stimulating state action on land use. The major federal stimulus was, of course, the anticipated funding for land use planning that would have been provided by the National Land Use Policy and Planning Assistance Act, proposed by the Nixon administration, Senator Henry Jackson, and Congressman Morris Udall. With the demise of that proposed

ix

national initiative, the future role of the federal government in encouraging state land use initiatives is much more clouded, and in turn, the likely rate and pattern of state innovation is more uncertain.

The author makes a number of policy recommendations on specific areas in which further federal action would be useful and desirable. It is our hope that this analysis will help to clear the air about the need for and probable impact of national land use legislation.

This study by Nelson Rosenbaum is one of a continuing series of reports on current land use issues, prepared under the direction of Worth Bateman of The Urban Institute's Land Use Center. It is being issued simultaneously with a complementary paper in the series, *The Law of the Land: Debating National Land Use Legislation 1970-75,* by Noreen Lyday. Read together, these two studies provide a comprehensive picture of legislative action on land use in the United States.

William Gorham
President
The Urban Institute

September 1976

Acknowledgments

The author is indebted to Worth Bateman, Director of the Land Use Center, for his assistance in formulating and guiding this research in innovative state land use legislation. Noreen Lyday, author of a companion study on national land use legislation, was a valuable source of ideas and information. Prue Larocca and Michael Fix served capably as research assistants in the often-tedious job of identifying and reviewing relevant statutes. The author is also grateful to a number of others who provided detailed comments and criticisms on the manuscript: J. Clarence Davies, Lawrence Susskind, Erwin Hargrove, Daniel Mandelker, and Robert Montjoy.

I. INTRODUCTION

THE REVOLUTION REVISITED

One of the most significant changes in intergovernmental relations over the last two decades has been state governments' reassertion of authority over the use of land.

Historically, except for federally owned lands, decisions on land use were delegated by the states to cities, counties, and towns. State governments confined themselves to passing enabling legislation which allowed local jurisdictions to plan, zone, and regulate the subdivision of land. In state capitals everywhere, land use problems were seen as local and urban matters, to be resolved without state intervention.

It was not until the sixties, when the alarming consequences of the postwar building boom rose to national attention and rural-dominated state legislatures gave way to more representative bodies, that conceptions about the appropriate role of state governments in land use decisionmaking began to change.

In 1961, the legislature of the then-new state of Hawaii took the first step in what Bosselman and Callies have termed "the quiet revolution in land use control" by adopting a statewide Land Use Law.[1] Under this law, a state Land Use Commission was directed to classify all of Hawaii's 6,424 square miles into urban, rural, agricultural, or conservation districts. The law gave the Hawaiian state government an unprecedented degree of control over the state's land resources.

During the next ten years, support for an increased state role in land use control began to spread. Scientists, conservationists, planners, lawyers, journalists, and ordinary citizens throughout the nation devoted an extraordinary amount of effort to exposing the economic, aesthetic, and environmental problems stemming from shortsighted and ineffective local control over land use. Solutions to such problems as protecting natural areas, siting low-income housing, and insuring adequate open space were increasingly viewed as beyond the scope or competence of local governments.

Encouraged by this new climate of opinion, several states began to enact innovative laws which, for the first time, gave state agencies direct control over one or more facets of land use policy. Notable among these pioneering states were California and Oregon in the West; Wisconsin and

---

1. Fred Bosselman and David Callies, *The Quiet Revolution in Land Use Control* (Washington, D.C., Council on Environmental Quality, 1971).

Minnesota in the Midwest; and Maine, Vermont, and Massachusetts in the East. By the end of 1971, when Bosselman and Callies published their analysis of innovations in state land use legislation enacted during the previous decade, they were able to conclude in an optimistic vein that reforms would continue to diffuse rapidly across the country.[2] Similar positive assessments of the strength of the land use reform movement and the likelihood of rapid and extensive adoption of new approaches by the states have been common in recent years.[3] However, even though reform of land use policy remains a topic of active study and debate in many states, numerous factors have combined during the last few years to dispel the vision of rapid nationwide acceptance of statutory innovations by state legislatures.

First, increased fuel costs have focused attention on the need to expand the discovery, extraction, and use of domestic energy resources, thus reducing the effectiveness of environmentalists' arguments for protection of natural areas. Indeed, the nation's belated recognition of domestic shortages in oil, natural gas, and important minerals threatens to weaken the environmentalist cause for years to come.

Second, recession-induced unemployment, high interest rates, and inflated costs have seriously depressed the building industry. Since 1973, the nation's politicians and economists have become increasingly concerned with finding ways to stimulate new construction rather than to regulate it at the state and federal levels.

Third, doubts have been raised about the constitutionality of the vigorous exercise of the states' police powers in protecting natural areas and open space. While proponents of reform have contended that arguments over the "takings issue" should be settled in the courts after a state has legislated its basic policy, opponents have capitalized on the legal uncertainties to delay or obstruct land use legislation based on the police power.

Finally, the prospect of land use regulation centralized at the state level has aroused a certain amount of ideological opposition from both conservatives and liberals. Within the United States, and in other countries as well, citizens have been expressing a growing skepticism about the ability of larger jurisdictions to solve sensitive social problems.

---

2. Bosselman and Callies, *Quiet Revolution*, op. cit., p. 327.

3. See, for example, William K. Reilly, ed., *The Use of Land: A Citizen's Policy Guide to Urban Growth* (New York, Thomas Y. Crowell Co., 1974); Council of State Governments, *The Land Use Puzzle* (Lexington, Ky., The Council, 1974); H. Milton Patton and Janet W. Patton, "Harbingers of State Growth Policies," 47 *State Government* 75 (1974); and Richard Krochalis, "State-wide Land Use Planning," 31 *Urban Land* 8 (1972).

These factors have clearly impeded the movement toward land use reform at the state level. During their 1974 sessions, seven state legislatures—Idaho, Iowa, Michigan, New Hampshire, Ohio, South Dakota, and Wisconsin—rejected proposals to expand state land use authority. In four states—Colorado, Maine, Maryland, and North Carolina—where new land use legislation was passed in 1974, the powers given to state governments were far weaker than those provided in the legislation of the pioneering states.[4] In Utah, in a referendum held in November 1974, the voters rejected a Land Use Act the legislature had approved. In Vermont, a comprehensive growth plan for the state, developed under the state's legislation of 1970 creating a Vermont Environmental Board, was rejected during both the 1974 and 1975 legislative sessions.

The impetus for reform at the federal level also appears to have weakened. The proposed Land Use Policy and Planning Assistance Act (S.268), which would provide federal funds for a variety of state-level land use activities hitherto unsupported by the federal government, failed to pass the 93rd Congress, and chances for passage of a related bill (S.984) in the current 94th Congress are quite remote. The Surface Mine Control and Reclamation Act of 1975 was vetoed by President Ford, and Congress failed to override. Funding for the HUD 701 planning program has been severely reduced.

Evidently, the strong nationwide momentum for state action on land use reform has subsided. Proposals for innovative land use legislation at the state level now confront a much more complex and difficult political struggle. For that reason, a more comprehensive understanding of the politics of land use legislation is vitally needed. Although many articles suggest sources of support for and opposition to state action,[5] and several studies of the legislative experience in individual states have been published,[6] there has as yet been no systematic examination of the overall pattern of state action on land use. Why are some state legislatures more receptive to innovations in land use policy than others? Does this receptiveness extend

---

4. In Colorado, for example, Gov. Richard Lamm called the statute (HB 1041) enacted by the legislature "an unworkable bill" because it failed to give the State Land Use Commission strong authority to regulate critical areas and activities. See *Land Use Planning Reports,* February 3, 1975.

5. See, for example, Frank J. Popper, "Land Use Reform: Illusion and Reality," *Planning,* September, 1974, 14-19; Richard Slavin, "An Interesting Beginning," 46 *State Government* 201 (1973); and James Coffin and Michael Arnold, eds., *A Summary of State Land Use Controls* (Washington, D.C., Plus Publications, 1974).

6. See, for example, Luther Carter, *The Florida Experience: Land and Water Policy in a Growth State* (Baltimore, Johns Hopkins University Press, 1974); Phyllis Myers, *Slow Start in Paradise* (Washington, D.C., The Conservation Foundation, 1974); and Phyllis Myers, *So Goes Vermont* (Washington, D.C., The Conservation Foundation, 1974).

to a wide variety of land use reforms, or is it restricted to comparatively narrow areas? Why do some kinds of innovation spread from state to state more rapidly than others? What are the states likely to do in the absence of new federal legislation? What are they likely to do if the federal Land Use Policy and Planning Assistance Act ever does become law?

The intent of this report is to provide, by answering these questions, a basic understanding of the scope and pace of land use reform across the nation. The hope is that the findings will prove useful to state legislators and legislative staff members interested in the background of reform proposals, members of Congress and federal administrators concerned with the need for national initiatives, and scholars and journalists interested in land use reform. The findings should also interest members of the many organizations which attempt to influence land use legislation at state and federal levels.

THE DIFFUSION OF INNOVATIVE LEGISLATION

An innovative legislative act can be defined, quite simply, as a statute which represents a distinct departure from past state practice—that is, it establishes a new state policy and program or extends an existing state policy and program into a novel area. This study systematically examines the origin and diffusion of nine innovative state statutes which vest state government with direct authority over land use. These nine statutes fall into three broad categories of reform: supervision of local growth management, siting of major facilities, and protection of natural areas. The diffusion of each of these innovations will be examined in relation to the pattern displayed by the other land use statutes as well as with respect to the general historical pattern of innovative legislative action among the states.

Recent studies of innovation and diffusion across a wide variety of state statutes show that the following patterns tend to characterize the spread of legislation:

A. Confirming popular perceptions about which states are "pioneers" and which are "laggards," empirical evidence demonstrates that it is the more populous, more affluent, more urbanized states that generally adopt innovative legislation first. In one study of eighty-eight innovative acts, the top five states on a composite index were New York, Massachusetts, California, New Jersey, and Michigan.[7] The states which scored lowest were Texas, South Carolina, Wyoming, Nevada, and Mississippi. Of course, any

---

7. Jack Walker, "The Diffusion of Innovations Among the American States," 63 *American Political Science Review* 880 (1969). Walker acknowledges that his composite scale is "crude" and "preliminary," because it does not test inter-item relationships (p. 888). Nonetheless, he utilizes it as the basic dependent variable.

4

composite index may mask numerous deviations from the general pattern, but other studies of different legislation confirm the dominance of the large industrialized states.[8] It is suggested that this receptivity to innovation is attributable to four major factors: 1) greater affluence leads to greater willingness to spend money on new programs,[9] 2) more competitive political systems in the larger states provide greater incentive for incumbents to be "progressive,"[10] 3) more extensive communication links and national contacts facilitate early awareness and discussion of innovative concepts,[11] and 4) the political culture of the larger states incorporates a desire for national legislative leadership.[12]

B. States within the same region of the nation tend to adopt particular innovations in a "cluster"—i.e., over a relatively short period of time.[13] Once one or two leading states within a region adopt an innovation, a process of intraregional comparison and emulation seems to take place that results in rapid adoptions by neighboring states. Diffusion thus tends to occur normally on a region-by-region basis. One observer explains the predominance of this regional pattern this way:

> The tendency of political leaders and government officials to acquire their cues from regional neighbors has several causes: the belief that neighbors have problems similar to one's own; the attitude among officials and interested citizens that it is "legitimate" to adapt one's programs to those of nearby government; and the structure of officials' organizational affiliations, which put them in frequent contact with counterparts in neighboring states.[14]

---

8. See, for example, Virginia Gray, "Innovation in the States: A Diffusion Study," 67 *American Political Science Review*, 1174 (1973). On Gray's composite index of innovativeness in education, civil rights, and welfare legislation, the top-ranked states are California, New York, Massachusetts, New Jersey, and Wisconsin. See also the rejoinder by Jack Walker, "Comment: Problems in Research on the Diffusion of Policy Innovations," 67 *American Political Science Review* 1186 (1973).

9. On the importance of affluence and industrialization in stimulating the willingness to spend more on state programs, see Richard Hofferbert, "Socio-Economic Dimensions of the American States: 1890-1960," 12 *Midwest Journal of Political Science* 401 (1968); Ira Sharkansky, "Economic Development, Regionalism, and State Political Systems," 11 *Midwest Journal of Political Science* (1968).

10. Duane Lockard, "State Party Systems and Policy Outputs," in Oliver Garceau, ed., *Political Research and Political Theory* (Cambridge, Harvard University Press, 1968); Ira Sharkansky and Richard Hofferbert, "Dimensions of State Politics, Economics and Public Policy," 63 *American Political Science Review* 867 (1969).

11. See Jack Walker, "The Diffusion of Knowledge and Policy Change: Toward a Theory of Agenda Setting," unpublished paper delivered at the 1974 Annual Meeting of the American Political Science Association, Chicago, September, 1974.

12. This point is emphasized by Walker, "Diffusion of Innovations," op. cit., p. 892.

13. Walker, "Diffusion of Innovations," op. cit.; Ira Sharkansky, *Regionalism in American Politics* (Indianapolis, Bobbs-Merrill, 1970).

14. Sharkansky, *Regionalism*, op. cit., pp. 12-13.

Certain types of innovative legislation transcend the region-by-region pattern and diffuse uniformly and simultaneously across the entire nation. Factors which tend to stimulate this "abnormal" pattern are 1) the commitment of a nationwide "social movement" of voluntary organizations to the spread of an innovation; 2) a very strong push from the federal government, either through publicity or legislation; 3) endorsement and support by relevant national professional organizations and governmental associations.

C. On the average, innovations in the statute law of the states require about twenty years to be adopted by the first twenty states.[15] Within this general pattern, two variants can be identified: 1) a slower "linear" diffusion rate, marked by a steady yearly increase in the total number of adoptions and 2) a faster "nonlinear" diffusion rate, characterized by an acceleration in the number of states adopting each year over time.[16] The slower linear diffusion rate tends to be associated with the "normal" region-by-region pattern. The faster rate tends to be associated with the nationwide diffusion pattern.

It is of interest to note that the two earliest innovations in state land use legislation—municipal zoning and municipal planning enabling legislation—display markedly different patterns of diffusion despite similarities in the origins of the innovations (Figure I-1).

In the case of zoning-enabling legislation, diffusion was nationwide, rapid, and nonlinear. California, New York, and Wisconsin first adopted statutes in 1917. By 1924, nineteen more states passed similar legislation, bringing the total to twenty-two in just seven years. By 1932, fifteen years after the first state enactment, forty-one of the forty-eight states had adopted the innovation.

Enabling legislation for municipal planning, on the other hand, spread in a gradual, linear manner on a region-by-region basis. Massachusetts was the first state to enact the statute in 1913. It was more than twenty years later when the legislation was enacted by the twentieth state.

The difference may be at least partly attributable to the fact that the federal government pushed its model zoning legislation (the Standard Zoning Enabling Act) much harder than its model planning statute (the Standard City Planning Enabling Act) and also that zoning legislation was strongly supported by a nationwide "movement" of lawyers and citizens groups.

The nine innovative statutes selected for analysis in this study share several common traits.

---

15. Walker, "Diffusion of Innovations," op. cit., p. 895.
16. Gray, "Innovation in the States," op. cit., pp. 1178-1182.

Figure I-1

DIFFUSION OF EARLY STATE LAND USE LEGISLATION

Municipal Zoning Enabling Legislation

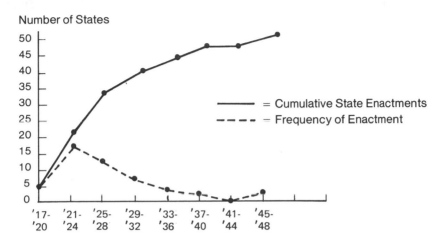

SOURCE: Housing and Home Finance Agency, *Comparative Digest of Municipal and County Zoning Enabling Statutes* (Washington, D.C.: Government Printing Office, 1952).

Municipal Planning Enabling Legislation

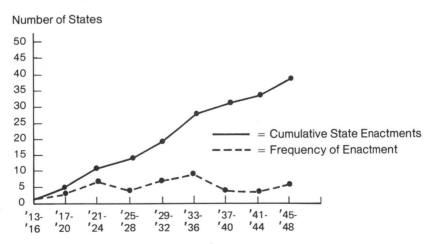

SOURCE: Derived from Housing and Home Finance Agency, *Planning Laws* (Washington, D.C.: Government Printing Office, 1957).

First, each involves the exercise of state police powers. There are, of course, other methods which state governments may use to exercise control over land use, including capital facilities budgeting, acquiring full-fee-simple or less-than-fee-simple title to land, and manipulating tax incentives and penalties. Innovative state legislation using these methods has been fairly common in recent years, and the subject may well deserve a study of its own. However, the major thrust of state action on land use has involved the initiation or expansion of direct police power control and supervision.

Second, each of the nine types of legislation has been enacted or favorably reported out to one of the legislative chambers in at least five states. Use of this criterion eliminated legislation peculiar to a particular state or too novel and controversial to have gained widespread legislative consideration.

Third, each of the types of legislation is potentially applicable to all 50 states. Some other varieties of land use legislation, such as regulation of unorganized areas, are of concern only to a minority of the states, and are therefore of limited interest. The innovations investigated here involve the most general issues of land use reform or include closely related statutes as a single type of innovative legislation ("wetlands protection," for instance, includes coastal wetlands, inland wetlands, and comprehensive wetlands legislation).

This study is organized as follows. Chapter II focuses upon innovative statutes which provide a new or expanded role for state agencies in supervising local control of development. The three statutes examined are mandatory local comprehensive planning, mandatory local subdivision control, and mandatory local zoning regulation. Chapter III involves new or expanded state control over the location of major facilities which have broad impacts beyond the particular locality in which they are situated. This includes the siting of power plants and transmission lines, large-scale industrial or commercial facilities, and surface mines. Chapter IV is concerned with the state role in preserving particularly fragile or valuable natural areas. Three types of legislation are examined: wetlands protection, shoreland and coastal zone management, and critical areas preservation. Finally, Chapter V provides a summary analysis of diffusion patterns across the full range of statutes, projects the future course of diffusion, and assesses the implications of these findings in relation to the need for further federal initiatives on land use.

II. GROWTH MANAGEMENT LEGISLATION

This chapter deals with the diffusion of legislation which expands the state role in the guidance and supervision of local growth management. Growth management, as used here, refers to the exercise of police power regulation by local government over the rate and location of new residential, commercial, and industrial development. Three types of innovative state legislation are examined:
1. Mandatory local comprehensive planning;
2. Mandatory local subdivision controls;
3. Mandatory local zoning regulation.

Reference to a state's adoption of one of these types of statutes means only that the legislature has required localities to plan, control subdivisions, or zone in accordance with some type of statewide standards and/or review. It does not imply any uniformity in the specific prerogatives and responsibilities assigned to state agencies in the implementation of legislative intent. Legislative enactments of the same basic innovation may differ widely in the allocation of authority to state government.

THE CRITIQUE OF LOCAL GROWTH MANAGEMENT

Following the widespread adoption of the basic planning and zoning enabling statutes by the states in the twenties and thirties, growth management was seen as the prerogative and responsibility of local governments. The sluggish pace of new land development in the Depression years of the thirties and the war years of the forties presented few challenges to test the capabilities of local land use regulatory systems. Through the early fifties, the way in which local governments exercised, or failed to exercise, their land use regulatory powers received little criticism.

In the postwar years, however, two major shifts in population—from southern and other rural areas to the major cities, and from the cities to suburbia—caused a dramatic increase in the demand for new residential, commercial, and industrial facilities. By the mid-fifties, the urban maladies which we experience today began to appear with increasing frequency—gross environmental degradation resulting from excessive concentration of industrial and commercial facilities, fiscal strain arising from overly rapid residential development, transportation problems stemming from unguided, sprawling growth, and social tensions resulting from residential segregation. Beginning among many of the professional groups heavily involved in land development, such as lawyers, planners, and architects, and spreading in the sixties to citizens organizations and the federal government, a broad critique of local growth management gradually developed. This critique had three major points.

The first was that state enabling statutes are permissive, thus allowing local governments to avoid exercising the land use control powers granted them by the state.[1] There was wide variation among the states in the degree to which local governments voluntarily enacted land use plans, zoning regulations, and subdivision ordinances, but the record in most states was very spotty.[2] As a consequence, growth was often merely displaced to neighboring territory rather than effectively managed. After deciding what to build and on what type of land, the developer could simply "shop around" for potential sites in communities with incomplete or nonexistent controls.

The second set of criticisms involved the poor quality of growth management efforts in many communities. Most state enabling statutes failed to require local governments to adhere to significant procedural or substantive standards.[3] Even in metropolitan areas where development pressures were greatest and local government budgets were largest, growth regulation was often exercised haphazardly and inconsistently.

One practice that incurred particularly harsh criticism was the exercise of regulatory controls without regard to a comprehensive land use plan.[4] Many jurisdictions with controls never developed such a plan in the first place; others simply ignored their existing plans in implementing zoning and subdivision regulations.

---

1. Among the numerous critics of the permissiveness of state enabling statutes, see in particular John Delafons, *Land Use Controls in the United States* (Cambridge, Mass., M.I.T. Press, 1962); Roger Cunningham, "Land Use Control—State and Local Programs," 50 *Iowa Law Review* 367 (1965); James Coke and John Gargan, *Fragmentation in Land Use Planning and Control* (Washington, D.C., National Commission on Urban Problems, Research Report No. 18, 1969).

2. The extent of variation between states in the scope of local coverage is extremely broad. In Indiana, for example, 80 percent of municipal land and 85 percent of county land has been zoned. More typical is Missouri, where 33 percent of municipal land and 11 percent of county land has been zoned. See the survey of land use controls coverage conducted by the Council of State Governments, reported in *The States' Role in Land Resource Management—Technical Appendix* (Lexington, Kentucky, Council of State Governments, 1972). See also the earlier, more comprehensive report by Allen Manvel, *Local Land and Building Regulation* (Washington, D.C., National Commission on Urban Problems, Research Report No. 6., 1968).

3. Delafons, *Land Use Controls,* op. cit., pp. 41-97; Richard Babcock, *The Zoning Game: Municipal Practices and Policies* (Madison, Wisconsin, University of Wisconsin Press, 1966); Daniel Mandelker, *The Zoning Dilemma* (Indianapolis, Bobbs-Merrill, 1971).

4. Charles Haar, "In Accordance With a Comprehensive Plan," 68 *Harvard Law Review* 1154 (1955); Allison Dunham, "A Legal and Economic Basis for City Planning," 58 *Columbia Law Review* 650 (1958); Norman Williams, "Development Controls and Planning Controls—The View from 1964," 19 *Rutgers Law Review* 86 (1964); John Rops, "Requiem for Zoning," in H. Wentworth Eldredge (ed.), *Taming Megalopolis* Volume II (New York, Praeger Publishers, 1967).

Another aspect of poor growth management procedure was the liberal and often arbitrary use of special devices, such as variances, conditional use permits, "floating" zones, and down-zoning. Although some flexibility is obviously essential in land use regulation, the proliferation and abuse of these devices helped weaken the predictability which is at the heart of effective growth management.[5]

In many communities, the quality of growth management was also diminished by the failure of public officials to involve the public in making sensitive land use decisions.[6] The reluctance of officials to inform, consult with, and account to the public systematically in either the planning or implementation of growth controls alienated not only black and other minority groups but also a wide spectrum of neighborhood citizen organizations interested in the quality of life in their communities. As a result of this deficiency, many communities manifested a chaotic record of growth management. The most sensitive cases frequently bypassed the established machinery and were decided by the courts or by mass citizen protests and political action.

The third major point made by the critics was that local growth management decisions were extremely parochial. Local officials rarely considered the effect of their land use decisions on neighboring communities. The typical state enabling statute did not require them to do so and provided no mechanism for mandatory coordination among local jurisdictions. Given the opportunity to ignore outside interests, many communities became "exclusivist," banning all types of land use not considered socially or economically desirable. Other communities took the opposite approach, encouraging any and all forms of growth, no matter how harmful the impact on surrounding areas.

Thus, with authority over land use dispersed among literally thousands of local governments throughout the nation, dealing with major problems such as pollution, transportation, and housing on an effective areawide

5. See, for example, "Zoning Variances and Exceptions: The Philadelphia Experience," 103 *University of Pennsylvania Law Review* 516 (1955); Richard Babcock, "The Chaos of Zoning Administration," *Zoning Digest* 12 (1960); "Zoning Variance Administration in Alameda County," 50 *California Law Review,* 101 (1962); Paul Black, "Administrative Procedure: The Stepchild of Zoning," 4 *Current Municipal Problems* 102 (1963).

6. Paul Davidoff. "Advocacy and Pluralism in Planning," 31 *Journal of the American Institute of Planners* 331 (1965); Alan Altshuler, *The City Planning Process* (Ithaca, N.Y., Cornell University Press, 1965); Clarence Davies, *Neighborhood Groups and Urban Renewal* (New York, Columbia University Press, 1966); Richard Babcock and Fred Bosselman, "Citizen Participation: A Suburban Suggestion for the Central City," 32 *Law and Contemporary Problems* 221 (1967). For an overview of the demand for citizen involvement in land use decisions, see Nelson Rosenbaum, *Citizen Involvement in Land Use Governance: Issues and Methods* (Washington, D.C., The Urban Institute, 1976).

basis (in other words, within a metropolitan region, a watershed, an air quality region, or a state) was extremely difficult.[7] In the absence of an areawide perspective on land use, critics questioned whether local growth controls were more helpful than harmful in enhancing public health, safety, and welfare.

TRADITIONAL STRATEGIES OF REFORM

Prior to the mid-sixties, advocates of fundamental reform in local growth management rarely attempted to achieve their goals through the enactment of innovative state laws. Instead, they concentrated on the more limited strategies of challenging local land use decisions in the courts and seeking voluntary areawide consultation and coordination.

Throughout the fifties and sixties, legal challenge to arbitrary, parochial, and corrupt local decisions was a favorite method of critics, and it remains in widespread use today. Unfortunately, as many reformers have realized, challenging land use decisions in the courts has several drawbacks.[8]

Legal battles are customarily expensive and lengthy; final verdicts may not be handed down for two or three years. Judges, it turns out, can be as arbitrary and capricious as local officials. And even when a verdict favorable to reform is handed down in an individual case, there is often considerable uncertainty about its standing as a precedent. Clearly, there have been certain cases in which the verdicts handed down by the highest state courts or the U.S. Supreme Court have been broadly applicable, thus serving the goal of fundamental reform.[9] But for every such case, there have

---

7. Charles Liebman, "Political Values and Population Density Control," 37 *Land Economics,* 347 (1961); Jon Krasnowiecki and James Paul, "The Preservation of Open Space in Metropolitan Areas," 110 *University of Pennsylvania Law Review* 179 (1961); Dennis O'Harrow and Jack Noble, "Intergovernmental Relations and Highway Planning: A Proposal," 16 *Zoning Digest* 193 (1964); Babcock, *The Zoning Game,* op. cit., 138-152; Lawrence Sager, "Tight Little Islands: Exclusionary Zoning, Equal Protection and the Indigent," 21 *Stanford Law Review* 767 (1969).

8. See Ira Heyman, "Legal Assaults on Municipal Land Use Regulation," in Marion Clawson (ed.), *Modernizing Urban Land Policy* (Baltimore, Johns Hopkins University Press, 1973); Daniel Fessler, "Casting the Courts in Land Use Reform Efforts: A Starring Role or a Supporting Part," in Clawson, *Modernizing Urban Land Policy,* op cit.

9. Two recent cases decided by the Oregon Supreme Court, for example, have accomplished many of the basic goals of reformers. In *Fasano* v. *Washington County Board of Commissioners* 507 P. 2d 23 (1973), the Court held that cities and counties must conform to strict procedural standards of notice, hearing, burden of proof, and findings of fact as well as the substantive standard of conformity to an adopted comprehensive plan in all re-zoning actions.
   In *Baker* v. *City of Milwaukie,* 533 P. 2d 772 (1975), the Oregon Supreme Court further ruled that all city zoning regulations must conform to a subsequently adopted comprehensive plan. See the commentary on these cases in Edward J. Sullivan and Laurence Kressel, "Twenty Years After—Renewed Significance of the Comprehensive Plan Requirement," 9 *Urban Law Annual* 33 (1975).

been scores of others in which the narrow grounds of the decision or the special circumstances of the case have limited their standing as a precedent. Given the amount of time and energy required, the wisdom of using the courts to accomplish the basically political tasks of growth management reform on a case-by-case basis is subject to growing doubt.

In addition to their courtoom activities, advocates of local growth management reform made strenuous efforts in the fifties and early sixties to stimulate voluntary regional cooperation and coordination by means of Councils of Government (COGs) and Regional Planning Councils (RPCs).[10] Councils of Government are voluntary associations of elected officials from a given set of jurisdictions, established either by local initiative or under state enabling legislation.[11] Regional Planning Councils are official agencies authorized by state legislation, ordinarily composed of private citizens appointed by the local governments involved.[12]

The creation of COGs and RPCs was greatly encouraged by passage of the Housing Act of 1954, because Section 701 of the act made federal funds available for comprenehsive regional planning. Under the prodding of such professional groups as the American Society of Planning Officials and the American Institute of Planners, and such organizations as the National Municipal League and the Regional Plan Association, the federal government progressively increased the funds available to these regional agencies. Along with the funds came increasing responsibilities for functional planning of federal programs, such as air and water pollution control. Nonetheless, the efforts of these regional agencies to improve cooperation and coordination in land use control among local governments did not get very far. Although a few examples of meaningful voluntary cooperation could be identified by the late sixties—for example, the "fair share" agreement for distribution of low-income housing reached by members of the Metropolitan Washington Council of Governments—the record of the COGs and RPCs

10. Warren Schmid, "The ABAG Case: Coordinating Common Problems in a Regional Setting" in Willis D. Harvey (ed.), *Where Governments Meet: Emerging Patterns of Intergovernmental Relations* (Berkeley, Calif., Institute of Governmental Studies, 1967); Washington Center for Metropolitan Studies, *Comprehensive Planning for Metropolitan Development* (Washington, D.C., The Center, 1970); Stanley Baldinger, *Planning and Governing the Metropolis: The Twin Cities Experience* (New York, Praeger, 1971); Royce Hanson, "Land Development and Metropolitan Reform," in Lowdon Wingo (editor), *Reform as Reorganization* (Washington, D.C., Resources for the Future, 1974).

11. Among the best general references on COGs are Royce Hanson, *Metropolitan Councils of Government,* (Washington, D.C., Advisory Commission on Intergovernmental Relations, 1966); Melvin Mogulof, *Governing Metropolitan Areas* (Washington, D.C., The Urban Institute, 1971).

12. On regional planning councils, see Council of State Governments, *Substate District Systems* (Lexington, Ky., The Council, 1971): Advisory Commission on Intergovernmental Relations, *Regional Decision Making: New Strategies for Substate Districts,* Chapters VII and VIII (Washington, D.C., G.P.O., 1973).

was generally mediocre.[13] By the late sixties, it appeared obvious that there was little prospect for fundamental reform of local growth management practices under the voluntary aegis of COGs and RPCs.

THE TURN TO THE STATES

Why was the potential role of state governments in improving local growth management practices ignored after the problems became evident? There were several obvious reasons.

Most of the development pressures and most of the abuses in growth management practices occurred in large metropolitan areas which had only the slimmest connections to state government. Under home rule charters and broad enabling legislation, most metropolitan jurisdictions made their own governmental decisions and resisted state intervention. The state seemed irrelevant to most urban problems in the fifties and much of the sixties. When urban governments needed help, they dealt directly with Washington without stopping at their state capitals.

Compounding the distance between state government and urban jurisdictions was the malapportionment of state legislatures. Over the years, many if not most of the state legislatures had become de facto rural governments, dominated by rural legislators, rural interests, and rural ways of doing things. The result was that those most interested in solving urban problems saw little point in becoming involved in state affairs. For good reason, urban and liberal advocates of land use and other urban reforms felt relatively powerless in state legislatures.[14] In addition, state agencies showed little capacity to supervise local growth management. State planning offices, in particular, were understaffed and weak. The likelihood of their taking a direct role in growth management seemed very remote.[15]

---

13. On the operation of the Metropolitan Washington COG, see Walter Scheiber, "Evolution of a COG: Tackling the Tough Jobs," 51 *Public Management* 10, (1969); and Walter Scheiber, "Regionalism: Its Implications for the Urban Manager," 31 *Public Administration Review* 42 (1971).

14. See Gordon Baker, *Rural Versus Urban Political Power* (New York, Doubleday, 1955); Paul David and Ralph Eisenberg, *Devaluation of the Urban and Suburban Vote*, (Charlottesville, University of Virginia, Bureau of Public Administration, 1961); William C. Havard and Loren P. Beth, *The Politics of Misrepresentation* (Baton Rouge, Louisiana University Press, 1962); Duane Lackard, *The Politics of State and Local Government* (New York, Macmillan, 1963)

15. See Institute on State Programming for the 70's, *State Planning: A Quest for Relevance* (Chapel Hill, N.C., The Institute, 1968); Thad Beyle, Sureva Seligson, and Deil Wright, "New Directions in State Planning," 35 *Journal of the American Institute of Planners* 334 (1969).

All of these problems began to change in the mid-sixties. One major reason was the precedent-setting *Baker* v. *Carr* verdict of 1962.[16] In that historic case, the Supreme Court held that the lower house of the Tennessee state legislature was unconstitutionally apportioned and made mandatory a new apportionment, giving many more seats in the legislature to urban areas. From that point onward, malapportioned state legislatures everywhere gradually gave way to more representative bodies with larger numbers of urban members. Gradually, the realization grew that urban areas could play a strong role in dealing with their problems through the states.

As the decade progressed, the shift in attitudes toward state governments precipitated by *Baker* accelerated as urban problems in housing, education, transportation, crime, and welfare reached a new intensity. After being scorned or ignored for decades, the states by 1970 were increasingly viewed as relatively stable and powerful instrumentalities of government, well-financed (with a few exceptions) by income and sales taxes, and capable of assuming a much more vigorous role in the federal system. Urban leaders began to look to the states more and more for financial and technical assistance, and federal officials seeking to implement the New Federalism increasingly focused upon the states as central components of American government.[17]

Of particular importance, federal grant programs which required statewide plans were coming into existence, thus stimulating a rapid expansion and improvement of state planning agencies.[18] With federal money available for state land use planning under the HUD 701 program as well as federal grants-in-aid for planning in transportation, education, health care, and recreation, the credibility of state supervision of growth management was greatly strengthened.

A final factor stimulating attention to the need for state action was the boom in rural land sales and second-home development. By the second half

---

16. *Baker* v. *Carr,* 369 U.S. 186 (1962). It was not until two years later that the Supreme Court decided that both houses of a state legislature must be based on the one man-one vote principle. *Reynolds* v. *Sims,* 84 S. Ct. 1362 (1964).

17. See, for example, Terry Sanford, *Storm over the States* (New York, McGraw Hill, 1967); Senator Edmund Muskie, "A Plea for Dynamic Federalism," 50 *Public Management* 161 (1968); Advisory Commission on Intergovernmental Relations, *Urban America and the Federal System* (Washington, D.C., G.P.O., 1969), Chapter 5. For an academic view of the states' resurgence, see Alan K. Campbell (ed.), *The States and the Urban Crisis* (Englewood Cliffs, N.J., Prentice Hall, 1970); and Ira Sharkansky, *The Maligned States* (New York, McGraw Hill, 1972).

18. Council of State Governments, *State Planning and Federal Grants* (Chicago, Public Administration Service, 1969); Richard Slavin, "The Expanding Dimensions of State Planning," in *Planning 1970* (Chicago, American Society of Planning Officials, 1971); Byle, Seligson, and Wright, "New Directions in State Planning," op. cit.

of the decade, the problems of guiding growth were no longer limited to major urban centers. Indeed, the inadequacies of the traditional system of local growth management were often most glaringly illustrated by the action (or inaction) of inexperienced rural jurisdictions in attempting to manage the spiraling demand for rural homes and recreational and industrial facilities.[19]

During the late sixties, a number of prominent studies and proposals revealed the shift in thinking among advocates of growth management reform. These books and reports aroused much public discussion and debate, and helped set the stage for the widespread consideration of innovative statutes by state legislatures.

One of the most prominent of these was Richard Babcock's *The Zoning Game,* published in 1967. Widely read, thanks to its clear, simple, and forthright style, Babcock's book advocated the expansion of state supervision and control over local growth management along three basic lines:

(1) more detailed statutory prescription of the required administrative procedures at the local level; (2) a statutory restatement of the major substantive criteria by which the reasonableness of local decision-making is measured; and (3) the creation of a statewide administrative agency to review the decisions of local authorities, with final appeal to an appellate court.[20]

Another work published in the same year that gained a wide audience was the study of options for growth management in Connecticut prepared by the American Society of Planning Officials.[21] Even though the ASPO study concentrated on a specific state, its recommendations were broad and generally applicable: (1) Local governments should be required to meet certain minimum planning requirements before being allowed to exercise land use regulation under the police power; (2) local governments should be required to meet certain minimum standards of fairness in the administrative procedures of land use controls; and (3) a state agency should be empowered to review and approve local plans and policies for compliance with state guidelines and should have the authority to adjudicate all disputes involving local land use decisions.[22]

These two works were complemented by a major study of the Advisory Commission on Intergovernmental Relations, entitled *Urban and Rural America: Policies for Future Growth.* The commission suggested that

---

19. See Department of Housing and Urban Development, *Urban Planning in Rural America* (Washington, D.C. G.P.O., 1968); President's Task Force on Rural Development, *A New Life for the Country* (Washington, D.C., G.P.O., 1970).

20. Babcock, *The Zoning Game,* op. cit., pp. 153-154.

21. American Society of Planning Officials, *New Directions in Connecticut Planning Legislation* (Chicago, ASPO, 1967)

22. Ibid., pp. 159-169.

the states should adopt legislation providing for

(1) coordination by an appropriate state agency of state, multi-county, metropolitan, and local planning and relating such planning to regional and national considerations; (2) conformance of programs and projects of state agencies to the state urbanization plan, and (3) formal review by an appropriate state agency for conformance with the state plan of metropolitan area and multi-county plans and of those local comprehensive plans, implementing ordinances, and projects having an impact outside the jurisdictions' borders.[23]

In 1969, the highly influential Final Report of the National Commission on Urban Problems (the Douglas Commission) followed.[24] On the basis of an exhaustive study of local growth management problems, the commission made two key recommendations:

. . .that state governments enact legislation denying land use regulatory powers after a reasonable period of time to local governments that lack a "development guidance program" as defined by state statute or administrative regulations made pursuant to such statute. Powers denied would be exercised by the state, regional, or county agencies as provided in the statute.[25]

. . .that each state create a state agency for planning and development guidance directly responsible to the Governor. The agency should exercise three types of functions: (1) research and technical assistance to localities in land use planning and control; (2) the preparation of state and regional land use plans and policies, and (3) *adjudication* and supervision of decisions by state and *local* agencies affecting land use. (Emphasis added.)[26]

As these books and reports were appearing, proposed articles of the influential American Law Institute Model Land Development Code were being circulated in draft form among government officials and within the professions concerned with land development. The institute's preparation of a comprehensive model statute began in 1963 with a grant from the Ford Foundation and support from the American Bar Association. It was prompted by the legal profession's discontent with the inadequacies and inconsistencies of local land use control.

The growth management reforms advocated in the ALI Model Code are not as sweeping as those proposed in some of the other studies. Most importantly, the Code rejects the idea of *requiring* local governments to plan or zone or control subdivisions. While conceding that such mandatory provisions might be desirable, the Code Reporter declares it inappropriate

---

23. Advisory Commission on Intergovernmental Relations, *Urban and Rural America: Policies for the Future Growth* (Washington, D.C., G.P.O., 1968), pp. 134-135.

24. National Commission on Urban Problems, *Building the American City* (Washington, D.C., G.P.O., 1969).

25. Ibid., pp. 237-238.

26. Ibid., p. 239.

for a state to force unwilling local governments to act.[27] The Code is similarly circumspect with reference to direct state supervision of local land use regulation, advocating the assertion of state authority only when "areas of critical concern" or "developments of regional impact" are involved.

However, at least with regard to comprehensive planning, the Code does make several proposals which support the more sweeping changes advocated elsewhere. First, the Code requires local comprehensive planning as a condition for the exercise of certain key regulatory powers given to local governments.[28] Second, the Code advocates an advisory review procedure which would allow a State Land Development Planning Agency to disapprove a local plan not in conformance with the state plan.[29] Third, the Code proposes the creation of a State Land Adjudicatory Board which would initially hear appeals from local land use decisions involving "areas of critical concern" and "developments of regional impact" but which could also be expanded into a general forum for the resolution of regulatory disputes over growth management.[30]

Although many other studies in more recent years have sustained the reform movement in its efforts to stimulate state action, it is clear that the five seminal works noted above marked a basic shift in the late sixties from emphasis on court action and voluntary regional cooperation to the passage of innovative growth management legislation at the state level. In many cases, one or more of these works directly set the agenda for consideration of innovative growth management legislation in state legislatures.

MANDATORY LOCAL COMPREHENSIVE PLANNING

Table II-1 shows the diffusion of state legislation mandating local comprehensive planning. The typical statute has two elements:

1. It requires all jurisdictions in the state which exercise land use regulatory powers to develop a comprehensive plan.
2. It establishes minimum statewide guidelines and standards which localities must meet in developing a plan.

The table lists all states which have included at least the two core elements in recent legislation.

---

27. American Law Institute, *A Model Land Development Code,* Proposed Official Draft No. 1 (Philadelphia, The Institute, 1974). See the commentary on Sections 2-101 and 3-101, pp. 37-38 and 142-143.

28. Ibid., Sections 2-210, 2-211, 2-212, 3-201, 4-102.

29. Ibid., Section 8-502.

30. Ibid., Sections 7-501 through 7-504.

TABLE II-1

DIFFUSION OF MANDATORY LOCAL
COMPREHENSIVE PLANNING LEGISLATION
(As of December 1975)

State	Year of Adoption	Statute
California	1965	Cal. Gov't. Code Ann. Sec. 65300 to 65307
Oregon	1969, 1973[1]	O.R.S. Sec. 215.050; 215.055; 215.505
Arizona	1971	A.R.S. Sec. 9-461 to 9-461.12; 11.802; 11.821
Colorado	1972	C.R.S. Sec. 30-28-106 to 30-28-116
Rhode Island	1972	General Laws R.I. Sec. 45-22-1 to 45-22-9
Nevada	1973	Nev. R.S. Sec. 278.030 to 278.265; 278.640 to 278.675
South Dakota	1974	South Dakota Code Sec. 11-2-2 to 11-2-12; 11-6-2
Virginia	1975	Virginia Code of 1950, Sec. 15.1-427 to 15.1-457
Idaho	1975	Local Planning Act of 1975, Idaho Code, Sec. 67-6501 to 67-6510
Wyoming	1975	State Land Use Planning Act, Wyo. S.A., Sec. 9-856, 9-857
Montana	1975	Montana Economic Land Development Act, R.C. of Mont., Sec. 84-7501 to 84-7526
Florida	1975	Local Government Comprehensive Planning Act, F.S.A., Sec. 163.3161 to 163.3211
Nebraska	1975	Laws 1975. L.B. 317. Jan. 21, 1975.

Proposed Legislation[2]

Iowa (Passed by House, tabled in Senate, 1975).

---

1. Initial legislation amended.
2. Reported out favorably to a full chamber during last two sessions.

The regional pattern discernible in Table II-1 is quite striking. Mandatory planning legislation is primarily a western phenomenon, beginning in 1965 with California—the leading regional state in population, industrialization, and affluence.[31] Seven of the twelve states which had followed California by December 1975 also are in the West. It is worth noting that Oregon, also a regional leader, was second after California, and that Colorado was fourth. Normal "regional emulation" seems to be the primary factor in the 1975 enactments by Idaho, Wyoming, and Montana, but the rapidity of these adoptions also seems to reflect unusual historical circumstances. Enormous growth pressures have developed recently in those states due to the extraction of surface coal and oil shale.

During 1975, Virginia and Florida became the first two southern states to adopt the legislation. Both states are regional leaders: Florida because of its recent population growth, Virginia because of historic traditions. Their enactment of planning statutes has already quickened interest elsewhere in the region. Under the mandate of the state's Land Policy Act of 1974, the North Carolina Land Policy Council is developing a land classification system and investigating the possible need for mandatory local planning. The Texas legislature also is studying the legislation, and further southern activity will be stimulated by the publicizing of growth management issues by the Southern Growth Policies Board.[32]

Outside the West and the South, only Nebraska and South Dakota in the Midwest and Rhode Island in the East have adopted the legislation. With the exception of Iowa, prospects for further action in the Midwest and Northeast seem less than favorable. Legislatures in such traditionally dominant states as New York, New Jersey, Massachusetts, Michigan, Wisconsin, and Ohio have yet to consider the legislation seriously. In part, the lack of activity reflects a substantial reduction of growth pressure in the East and Midwest as well as the fact that most urban governments in these states already have plans in place.[33] In addition, these states have effective concentrations of large urban jurisdictions which typically resist the imposition of state standards and guidelines in any area of policy. Finally, particularly tight budget conditions in the Northeast and Midwest have made state governments reluctant to appropriate new funds for planning activities or to

---

31. On the origins and requirements of the California legislation, see California Council on Intergovernmental Relations, *General Plan Guidelines* (Sacramento, The Council, 1973); Planning and Conservation Foundation, *Land and the Environment: Planning in California Today* (Los Altos, William Kaufmann, 1975).

32. See Commission on the Future of the South, *The Future of the South* (Raleigh, N.C., Southern Growth Policies Board, 1974, pp. 69-72.

33. See Council of State Governments, *The State's Role. . .Technical Appendix,* op. cit., for a comparison of the percentage of urban jurisdictions with controls across the states.

require local governments to do so.[34] This reluctance has been strengthened by uncertainty over the future funding levels of the federal Department of Housing and Urban Development's Section 701 planning assistance program and the demise of proposed National Land Use Policy and Planning Assistance Act.

The rate of diffusion, thirteen states over ten years, is within the average range. Adoptions accelerated to six in 1975, but these were mostly concentrated in one region. At this point, the pattern of diffusion remains essentially "normal"—adoptions are clustered among neighboring states in a single region and are relatively steady from year to year. Mandatory planning may, however, be on the verge of a breakthrough into a more rapid, nationwide, nonlinear pattern.

MANDATORY LOCAL SUBDIVISION CONTROL

Many of the worst cases of corruption, arbitrariness, and parochialism identified by critics of local growth management have involved subdivision control. The subdivision of land into building lots is the basis of most new residential construction in the United States and plays a crucial role in the overall pattern of urban growth. The law of most states requires that plats of proposed subdivisions be submitted to local governing bodies for approval before lots are officially recorded and offered for sale to the public. However, the laws seldom set criteria which local governing bodies must use in reviewing subdivision platting proposals, nor do they require the preparation of an explicit subdivision control ordinance.[35] The result is often arbitrary and inconsistent decisionmaking that shifts with the political winds. It is not surprising that so many subdivision cases end up in court.

Table II-2 presents the data on the diffusion of legislation which attempts to overcome the deficiencies of the traditional approach. The typical mandatory subdivision control statute consists of two parts:

1. It provides that all municipalities and/or counties must actively regulate subdivisions *in accordance with an ordinance.*
2. It provides for a set of substantive state standards and guidelines for the development of such ordinances.

Some statutes include an additional section providing for direct review or appeal of local subdivision control decisions at the state level. However,

---

34. In Michigan, for example, cost has been a major consideration in preventing a major land use bill which includes mandatory local planning (H.4234, 1975) from being reported out of committee. See *Land Use Planning Reports,* March 10, 1975, p. 9.

35. See Cunningham, "Land Use Control," op. cit., pp. 415-437; J. Reps and B. Smith, "Control of Urban Land Subdivision," 14 *Syracuse Law Review* 405 (1963).

TABLE II-2

DIFFUSION OF MANDATORY LOCAL
SUBDIVISION CONTROL LEGISLATION
(As of December 1975)

State	Year of Adoption	Statute
California	1971, 1974[1]	The Subdivision Map Act. Cal. Gov't. Code Ann. Sec. 66410 to 66499.37
Arizona	1971	A.R.S., Sec. 11-806.01
Colorado	1972	C.R.S. Sec. 30-28-133
Oregon	1973	O.R.S. Sec. 92.010 to 92.245
Nevada	1973	Nev. R.S. Sec. 278.320 to 278.495
New Mexico	1973	New Mexico Subdivision Act, N.M.S.A. Sec. 70-3-9, 70-5-1 to 70-5-29
Idaho	1975	Local Planning Act of 1975. Idaho Code Sec. 67-6513, 67-6514
Virginia	1975	Virginia Code of 1950, Sec. 15.1-465 to 15.1-483
Wyoming	1975	Wyo. S.A. Sec. 18.289.10 to 18.289.24
Nebraska	1975	Laws 1975, L.B. 317, Jan. 21, 1975

Proposed Legislation[2]
Iowa (Passed by House, tabled in Senate, 1975).

---

1. California first required all localities to develop subdivision control ordinances in 1953, but it was not until 1971 that the law was amended to incorporate substantive statewide standards and guidelines. A new comprehensive statute, incorporating and superseding the old amended law, was enacted in 1974.

2. Reported out favorably to a full chamber during last two sessions.

as in the case of mandatory planning legislation, such a provision is more a matter of intergovernmental relations than a fundamental component of the innovation. The table lists all states whose law incorporates the two essential reforms: control by ordinance and statewide standards.

The regional pattern illustrated in Table II-2 is similar to that in Table II-1. It is the states of the West that dominate reform of subdivision controls.

Once again, California initiated the innovation and was soon followed by two other regional leaders, Colorado and Oregon. Outside the West, only two states have adopted the innovation.

Diffusion has been relatively rapid. Ten states have promulgated mandatory local subdivision controls over a five-year period. Four of the ten adoptions occurred in 1975, indicating accelerating interest. This rapidity is at least partially attributable to the fact that mandatory subdivision control is an "incremental" innovation. Ordinarily, local governments already have some kind of existing subdivision control procedures in place. Imposing a requirement for ordinances based on state standards is a significant but logical extension of existing practice. Furthermore, given existing controls, the cost of the innovation is likely to be small. State legislators can thus take credit for "doing something" about the problem of rapid residential growth without imposing major new expenses on state or local government. Legislative consideration of the innovation is therefore free of domination by budgetary considerations which characterize debate on the other aspects of growth management reform.

MANDATORY LOCAL ZONING REGULATION

The most controversial innovation in state reform of local growth management is legislation making local zoning mandatory. The controversy is not hard to understand, because zoning is the keystone of local land use control. The state zoning laws enacted so far are more diverse than the mandatory planning or subdivision ordinances, but they share at least two common elements which constitute the core of the innovation:

1. They provide (with lesser and greater degrees of direct state involvement) for zoning regulation of the entire land area of the state by local governments.
2. They provide (with lesser and greater degrees of latitude) for state policy guidelines and/or supervision of zoning regulation by state agencies.

Table II-3 shows that, as with the previous statutes, it is the western states which demonstrate the greatest receptivity. All but one of the states which have mandatory local zoning statutes are in the West. Oregon originated the innovation in 1969 and was followed by California. In accord with the pattern of regional emulation, the next to adopt were Nevada, Arizona, and Idaho. Nevada's statute does not directly require counties to zone the land under their jurisdiction, but if they do not implement zoning regulations by July 1, 1975, the governor's office will preempt their authority and zone for them. In Idaho, all counties and municipalities are required to zone in accordance with a comprehensive plan that comes under state review and

23

TABLE II-3
DIFFUSION OF MANDATORY LOCAL
ZONING LEGISLATION
(As of December 1975)

State	Year of Adoption	Statute
Oregon	1969, 1973[1]	O.R.S. Sec. 215.050; 215.055; 215.505
California	1970[2]	Cal. Gov't Code Ann. Sec. 65910 to 65912
Nevada	1973.	Nev. R.S. Sec. 278.640 to 278.675
Arizona	1974	A.R.S., Sec. 11-821 to 11-821.01
Idaho	1975.	Local Planning Act of 1975, Idaho Code, Sec. 67-6511 to 67-6529
Nebraska	1975.	Laws 1975, L.B. 317, Jan. 21, 1975

Proposed Legislation[3]
Iowa (Passed by House, tabled in Senate, 1975)

---

1. Initial legislation amended.

2. California's law requires all counties and municipalities to zone land under their jurisdiction into two categories—open space and other. It is thus more limited than the other statutes, which require zoning under a wide range of categories.

3. Reported out favorably to a full chamber during last two sessions.

Arizona's statute is similar. Nebraska, a midwestern state with close ties to the West, also adopted a statute in 1975.

The rate of diffusion of this statute is somewhat slower than that of the other growth management legislation. The innovation has diffused on an average linear pattern—six adoptions over six years. This grudging acceptance contrasts markedly with the rapid nationwide diffusion of zoning enabling legislation in the twenties. Several factors have retarded the progress of mandatory zoning laws.

First, there is widespread resistance among conservative and rural legislators to the principle of zoning itself. Nonurbanized areas have traditionally shunned the use of zoning for land use control.[36] Of course, mandatory comprehensive planning and mandatory subdivision control legislation encounter similar ideological resistance, but the opposition is not so vigorous nor so united because planning does not necessarily involve regulation, and subdivision control does not incorporate any permanent restrictions on particular tracts of land. Urban and suburban legislators in most legislatures might be able to pass mandatory zoning legislation over the ideological objections of rural conservative forces, but they are themselves constrained by the disinclination of their local constituencies to subject zoning actions to state guidelines and/or review. Zoning, after all, has been the major tool for maintaining exclusive neighborhoods in suburban areas. Subjecting the use of this tool to external supervision has been bitterly resisted by many communities, as reaction to court decisions on fair housing has demonstrated. Thus, even the suburban legislator who favors the innovation may tread cautiously for fear of outdistancing his or her constituency.

A second factor discouraging diffusion is the cost and cumbersomeness of zoning as a tool of land use control. Zoning requires a substantial bureaucracy to prepare ordinances, enforce regulations, and prepare for hearings on zoning changes, variances, conditional use permits, and so forth. State guidelines and/or review make local zoning administration even costlier. Zoning is also cumbersome in terms of the time required for decisionmaking and the frequency of legal challenges. Intricate litigation may tie up legal staff for years. In a time of budgetary crisis, there is thus concern among state legislators about forcing localities to expend additional funds on zoning regulation. Although state legislatures can choose to defray all or part of the additional cost of mandatory zoning, few seem interested now in new programs which require substantial state spending. As with mandatory planning legislation, the reduction of the HUD 701 program and the demise of proposed national land use legislation have clouded the potential federal contribution to the costs of local zoning.[37]

The final factor which has impeded rapid acceptance of the innovation is growing discontent among professionals with the "negativism" of zoning.

---

36. The differing attitudes of rural and urban jurisdictions can be seen, for example, in Ohio. In that state, 98 percent of the cities have zoned the land under their jurisdiction. The corresponding figures for rural areas are 48 percent of the townships, 41 percent of the villages, and 13 percent of the counties. See Department of Economic and Community Development, "Local Land Use Controls in Ohio: Their Extent and Effectiveness" (Columbus, Ohio, Ohio Land Use Policy Work Group, December 1974).

37. In Washington State, for example, a mandatory local planning and zoning bill (H. 168, 1975) was tabled in committee due to the lack of federal financial support for the proposed activities. See Land Use Planning Reports, April 14, 1975.

Zoning is a passive and reactive method of land use control that is quite manipulable. All of the prohibitions written into zoning ordinances and maps are subject to challenge and change. The initiative lies with the developer and property owner. Zoning does nothing to foster the kind of development a community wants. At best, it leaves the door ajar for creative land development. Planners, architects, lawyers, and others frustrated with the limitations of zoning have suggested a wide variety of novel techniques for "positive" control of land use, from purchase of development rights to capital facilities budgeting to tax incentives.[38] Experimentation with these new techniques has diverted much attention from zoning. On the other hand, zoning has established its effectiveness by at least discouraging, if not halting, certain types of development. This record is the primary source of strength for the innovation. For a state faced with substantial growth pressures, mandated zoning regulation on a statewide basis may be the only sure way to slow the pace of development.

CONCLUSION

All three types of growth management legislation discussed in this chapter—comprehensive planning, subdivision control, and zoning regulation—have found their widest approval in the West. Table II-4 shows that eight of the thirteen states which have adopted mandatory planning legislation are in the West. The two midwestern states which have also acted, Nebraska and South Dakota, are in many ways aligned with the West. Of the ten states which have adopted subdivision controls, only Virginia and Nebraska are outside the West. Of the six states which have adopted zoning regulation, all are in the West except Nebraska. While the various reforms of local growth management remain an active topic of discussion in state legislatures in other parts of the country, formal legislative proposals were rarely reported out of committee there during 1974 and 75.

The receptiveness of the western states to these types of legislation can be attributed to three factors:

1. Over the last decade, the western states as a group have been the scene of the greatest land development pressures and have suffered some of the worst abuses in land speculation and rapid, slipshod land development.
2. Although local autonomy is strong in the West, state government traditionally has dominated the politics of those states. And, except

---

38. The most comprehensive analysis of nonregulatory techniques for growth management is found in Randall Scott (ed.), *Management and Control of Growth, Volumes II and III* (Washington, D.C., The Urban Land Institute, 1975).

TABLE II-4

SUMMARY STATISTICS:
DIFFUSION OF GROWTH MANAGEMENT LEGISLATION

Adoption Information	TYPE OF LEGISLATION		
	Mandatory Local Comprehensive Planning	Mandatory Local Subdivision Controls	Mandatory Local Zoning Regulation
Date of First Adoption	1965	1971	1969
Total Number of Adoptions	13	10	6
Most Adoptions in One Year	6 (1975)	4 (1975)	2 (1975)
Adoptions by Region			
Northeast	1	0	0
South	2	1	0
Midwest	2	1	1
West	8	8	5

for California, those states have few major urban areas which might challenge the prerogatives of state government.

3. Except in zoning regulation (where Oregon was the first state and California the second), California was the first state to adopt growth management reforms. California's importance, both nationally and regionally, made diffusion throughout the West a certainty.

Of the three types of legislation, mandatory comprehensive planning has proved to be the most acceptable, with thirteen adoptions in ten years. Six of the thirteen occurred in 1975. Zoning regulation has been the least acceptable, averaging one state adoption per year.

Table II-5 shows the time interval, in years, between adoption by the first state (designated 0) and adoption by other states. From this table, it can be seen that states which have adopted one of the innovations relatively early also tend to adopt one or both of the others early. California is

27

clearly the most innovative state, followed by Oregon, Arizona, and Colorado. These findings tend to bear out the proposition discussed in Chapter I that the largest, most affluent, and industrialized states within each region are typically most receptive to innovation.

TABLE II-5

**SUMMARY STATISTICS: STATE ACTION ON
GROWTH MANAGEMENT LEGISLATION
(Time Interval Since First Adoption, in Years)**

State	Mandatory Local Comprehensive Planning	Mandatory Local Subdivision Control	Mandatory Local Zoning Regulation
Alabama	—	—	—
Alaska	—	—	—
Arizona	6	0	5
Arkansas	—	—	—
California	0	0	1
Colorado	7	1	—
Connecticut	—	—	—
Delaware	—	—	—
Florida	10	—	—
Georgia	—	—	—
Hawaii	—	—	—
Idaho	10	4	6
Illinois	—	—	—
Indiana	—	—	—
Iowa	—	—	—
Kansas	—	—	—
Kentucky	—	—	—
Louisiana	—	—	—
Maine	—	—	—
Maryland	—	—	—
Massachusetts	—	—	—
Michigan	—	—	—
Minnesota	—	—	—
Mississippi	—	—	—
Missouri	—	—	—
Montana	10	—	—
Nebraska	10	4	6

(Continued)

TABLE II-5 (Continued)

State	Mandatory Local Comprehensive Planning	Mandatory Local Subdivision Control	Mandatory Local Zoning Regulation
Nevada	8	2	4
New Hampshire	—	—	—
New Jersey	—	—	—
New Mexico	—	2	—
New York	—	—	—
North Carolina	—	—	—
North Dakota	—	—	—
Ohio	—	—	—
Oklahoma	—	—	—
Oregon	4	2	0
Pennsylvania	—	—	—
Rhode Island	7	—	—
South Carolina	—	—	—
South Dakota	9	—	—
Tennessee	—	—	—
Texas	—	—	—
Utah	—	—	—
Vermont	—	—	—
Virginia	10	4	—
Washington	—	—	—
West Virginia	—	—	—
Wisconsin	—	—	—
Wyoming	10	4	—

III. SITING LEGISLATION

Since the early sixties, the use of land for major developments such as electric power plants, manufacturing facilities, and surface mines has aroused increasing opposition. Starting with the original *Scenic Hudson* case, a large proportion of the environmental litigation of the past decade has involved attempts to halt the development of various types of industrial facilities.[1] Partly as a result of the nation's increased environmental awareness and partly as a response to the success of environmental and citizen organizations in thwarting such developments, the procedures for regulating the location of major facilities have come under scrutiny. State legislatures have responded to the problem by enacting innovative statutes which either broaden the powers of state agencies to supervise local land use decisions on siting or shift direct decisionmaking authority to the state level.

This chapter examines the diffusion of three kinds of legislation that gives states new or expanded powers over the location of major facilities:

1. Electric power plants and transmission lines;
2. Large-scale industrial and commercial facilities; and
3. Surface mines.

As in the previous chapter, reference to a state's adoption of one of these statutes does not imply any uniformity in the allocation of prerogatives between state and local governments.

THE CRITIQUE OF LOCAL SITING DECISIONS

The conflict over the siting of major facilities is unusual among land use issues in that the major protagonists in the controversy share common ground on at least one point—namely, that local governments lack the perspective and resources necessary to make sound decisions on the location of large developments.

From the viewpoint of developers and industrialists, local governments seem all too vulnerable to the views of highly organized environmental groups and community associations that oppose development

---

1. *Scenic Hudson Preservation Conference* v. *FPC*, 354 F. 2d 608 (2d Cir. 1965), 453 F. 2d 463 (2d Cir. 1971). For an overview of environmental litigation over the last decade, see Joseph Sax, *Defending the Environment* (New York, Knopf, 1970); Frederick Anderson, *NEPA in the Courts* (Baltimore, Md., Johns Hopkins University Press, 1973); Jerome Rose (ed.), *Legal Foundations of Environmental Planning* (New Brunswick, N.J., Center for Urban Policy Research, 1974).

without regard for economic objectives.[2] Local governments have made a marked departure from past practice when they generally supported all types of land development that would increase jobs and tax rolls. Although developers and industrialists instinctively oppose greater governmental intervention in land development decisions, they have gradually recognized that without some form of advance planning and designation of desirable locations by higher level jurisdictions, it is increasingly uncertain whether major environmentally sensitive facilities can be developed. Thus, there is evidence of growing support in recent years for a more positive, more assertive state posture on major facility siting. The Northern States Power Company, for example, actively supported the development of a state program for power plant siting in Minnesota after experiencing several frustrating battles with local governments over the location of a new generating facility.[3] Under this program, established in 1973, the state, with the cooperation of power companies, has prepared an inventory of acceptable plant sites from which locations can be selected with some degree of confidence that a generating facility can be expeditiously developed.

From the viewpoint of citizens concerned with the environmental, social, and/or fiscal impacts of major facility development, on the other hand, local governments still seem all too willing to turn a blind eye to broader long-term effects in a shortsighted effort to raise additional property tax revenues.[4] This necessitates costly and continual "firefights" against proposals deemed particularly harmful. Environmental and community groups have had substantial success in obstructing or delaying major projects through legal challenge both on local and higher levels of review, but such efforts are difficult to sustain over an extended period. There is also the serious question of whether broad environmental and social

---

2. For the reaction of developers and industrialists to some major local siting controversies, see Charles F. Luce, "Power for Tomorrow: The Siting Dilemma," 1 *Environmental Law* 60 (1970); Oliver Woods et al., *The BASF Controversy Employment* v. *Environment* (Columbia, S.C., University of South Carolina Bureau of Business and Economic Research, Essays in Economics No. 25, 1971); "Voters Reject Refinery Plant in St. Mary's," *The Washington Post,* July 24, 1974; "Durham, N.H. Rejects Onassis Refinery Plan," *The New York Times,* Mary 7, 1974.

3. See R.W. Comstock, "Open Planning and Power Plant Siting," paper delivered to Westinghouse International School for Environmental Management, Fort Collins, Colo., July 1975 (available from Northern States Power Company, Minneapolis, Minn.).

4. See William K. Reilly (ed.), *The Use of Land: A Citizen's Policy Guide to Urban Growth* (New York, Thomas Crowell, 1973), Chapter I; U.S. Citizen's Advisory Committee on Environmental Quality, *Citizens Make the Difference: Case Studies of Environmental Action* (Washington, D.C., G.P.O., 1973); Nelson Rosenbaum, *Citizen Involvement in Land Use Governance: Issues and Methods* (Washington, D.C., The Urban Institute, 1976).

goals are best achieved through an essentially negative, adversary approach. Banning a major facility in one community does not mean that it will not be built elsewhere. Typically, the facility is merely displaced to a neighboring community that is less well-organized and less capable of effectively controlling the impacts of development. As one environmental lawyer notes, "In the process, developers of the private sector. . .employ siting methods which are essentially opportunistic in that the methods are designed to identify paths of least resistance from interest groups irrespective of the environmental consequences associated with the sites under consideration."[5] The result of displacement may ultimately be greater environmental, fiscal, or social strain than would have occurred in the original area.

As an alternative to the ad hoc adversary approach, many environmentalists have therefore advocated more systematic and comprehensive means of incorporating environmental and social considerations into the site decision process. One major thrust is support for state and local acts which require the preparation of an environmental impact statement for all major regulatory decisions. Impact analysis typically includes explicit identification and evaluation of alternatives to a particular proposal. Decisionmakers thus are provided with some sense of the positive options available in a particular case. But, as many have realized, impact analysis is not a substitute for advance planning. State and local decisionmakers are not required to heed the environmental, social, or fiscal effects revealed by impact analysis in making regulatory decisions.[6] Thus, many environmentalists and conservation organizations have also supported the concept of systematic advance planning and identification of sites for major facilities. There is considerable uneasiness among environmentalists about state or

---

5. Michael Baran, "Environmental Decision-Making and the Siting of Facilities," 5 *Environmental Law Reporter* 50089 (1975).

6. On the utilization of environmental impact statements in the decisionmaking process, see Thomas Muller, "State Mandated Impact Evaluation; A Preliminary Assessment," (Washinton, D.C., The Urban Institute, Contract Report 0217-01, February 1976). Muller notes, for example, with reference to the effect of impact analysis requirements in Florida, "Interviews with each of the ten Broward and Leon County supervisors indicated that a large majority felt the DRI process had no effect or only a small effect on their land use decision" (p.33). See also K. Christensen, D. Keyes, P. Schaenman and T. Muller, "State Required Impact Evaluation of Land Developments," (Washington, D.C., The Urban Institute, Working Paper 214-02, July 1974).

It should be noted, however, that the courts have become increasingly willing to intervene in the substance of agency decisionmaking to insure "adequate consideration" of all affected interests specified in environmental impact statements. See *Calvert Cliffs Coordinating Committee* v. *AEC*, 449 F.2d 1109 (Washington, D.C. Cir. 1971). An evaluation of the evolution and implementation of the adequate consideration doctrine under NEPA and related state statutes may be found in Richard Stewart, "The Reformation of American Administrative Law," 88 *Harvard Law Review* 1669 (1975).

regional preemption of local decisions, but it is recognized that local governments simply do not have the scope or competence to undertake responsibility for both protecting the environment and encouraging the development of needed facilities.[7]

Like the developers and the citizen groups, those within the professional community of planners, economists, and lawyers also find existing procedures inadequate when it comes to selecting sites for large-scale developments. Major industrial and commercial facilities, power plants, surface mines, and so forth are key factors in a state's economic development. Under present procedures, these vital sectors of economic development are left to the discretion of local governments which are often unaware of and unprepared to evaluate the need for prospective large-scale developments. Except in large urban jurisdictions which have their own economic development agencies, local governments typically respond to siting proposals in an ad hoc manner, making decisions without the benefit of policy guidance on desirable locations for major facilities and without having considered broader interests. In the view of many professionals, local governments should not be allowed to block necessary and desirable development on an arbitrary basis, nor should they be allowed to authorize any and all developments regardless of their broader regional and statewide impacts. Both advance planning of major facility development areas and statutory sanction for state supervision of siting matters are thus supported. For example, the ALI's Model Land Development Code advocates creation of a State Land Adjudicatory Board which would be empowered to assess the overall balance of costs and benefits and to make a final decision on the siting of "developments of regional impact."[8] The board would be explicitly authorized to preempt local judgments on developmental proposals, if necessary.

Another major criticism of existing arrangements which underlies the advocacy of state authority over siting relates to the multiple and overlapping environmental certifications which projects must obtain from different agencies and levels of government. In addition to the approval needed to use the land, numerous permits relating to health, conservation, pollution, water supply, etc., must be obtained at local, state, and federal levels before construction can actually progress. This fragmented approach leaves major projects at the mercy of the most narrowly drawn criteria and forces applicants to conform to often conflicting or contradictory standards.

---

7. See Reilly, *The Use of Land*, op. cit., pp. 203-205.

8. The American Law Institute, *A Model Land Development Code* (Philadelphia, The Institute, 1974), Proposed Official Draft No. 1, Article 7, Sections 7-501 through 7-504.

Although some developers and industrialists have indicated support for federal preemption of state and local regulation, particularly in the fields of energy development and production, most attention has focused on the need for a "one-stop clearinghouse" at the state level.[9] Most of the clearances typically required for major facilities, such as wetlands or shorelands permits, fish and wildlife licenses, and health and safety approvals, are established under state legislation in the first place. The states also play the central operational role in enforcement of federal air, water, and radiation pollution standards and hold ultimate authority over the environmental standards imposed by local government ordinances. There is thus substantial support among developers for creation of a unified permitting process at the state level.

There has been some opposition among community and environmental groups to "one-stop" environmental certification, but many environmental advocates—particularly in the professional communities—agree that agency-by-agency approval has been a serious problem. The ABA Special Committee on Environmental Law, for example, is highly critical of "an institutional setting of overlapping regulatory regimes, conflicting jurisdictional claims between levels of government and between different agencies on the same level."[10] These conflicts and overlaps impede a clear overall assessment of the environmental costs of major facilities. The committee strongly recommends the creation of a unified siting agency on the state level with the authority to consolidate the verdicts of the various agencies into a comprehensive environmental judgment.

THE AGENDA OF REFORM

In contrast to proposals for reform of local growth management procedures, efforts to transform siting procedures came to prominence sequentially rather than simultaneously, in response to different events and conditions: first power plant siting, then large-scale development siting, and finally surface mine siting. In each case, however, at least one common element is shared: the key factor in setting the agenda for consideration of reform by the states was proposed federal legislation.

---

9. See Harold Wise, "A One-Stop Center for State-Required Permits Related to Land Use and Environmental Concerns," (Washington, D.C., Harold Wise and Associates, Working Paper, February 28, 1974); William Masterson, "Coordinated Permits: The Washington Experience," *Environmental Comment*, October 1975, pp. 5-10; "IDRC Airs Views on Environmental and Land Use Controls," *Industrial Development*, May/June 1975.

10. Special Committee on Environmental Law, American Bar Association, *Industrial Development and the Environment: Legal Reforms to Improve the Decision-Making Process in Industrial Site Selection* (Chicago, The American Bar Association, Review Draft, August 1, 1973), p. I-2.

Power Plants

The need to reform procedures for the siting of new electric generating plants and transmission lines first came to national attention in the mid-sixties. The acceleration of concern was stimulated by the great Northeastern power failures of 1965 and 1967, which first made the nation aware that its power supply might be insufficient. The ensuing period of brownouts, intentional service cutoffs, and voltage reductions along with disputes over the siting of nuclear power plants stimulated intense interest in the reliability and environmental effects of power generation and transmission across the country.

The initial focus of reform efforts in the 1967-68 period was expanding the planning and regulatory powers of regional and federal agencies. In 1967, after an extensive study by the FPC, the Johnson administration submitted to Congress the proposed Electric Power Coordinating Act.[11] This legislation increased the authority of the FPC to plan and license high voltage transmission lines and to order interconnections between utilities. The bill also provided for establishment of regional councils of utilities to coordinate advance planning for the construction and operation of generating facilities and transmission lines. No role was provided for the states. Although considered in Congress each year from 1967 through 1970, the proposed legislation was consistently rejected in committee. The key factor in the defeat of this approach was the failure to address explicitly the resolution of conflicts between environmentalists and utilities over siting of facilities.

In 1969 and 1970, as environmental conflicts intensified and efforts to increase the authority of federal and regional agencies were rejected by Congress, the focus of reform gradually shifted to the states.

First, several states began to act on their own initiative to resolve siting problems. In 1969, Vermont became the first state to establish state-wide land use criteria for the siting of power plants and transmission lines and to vest its existing Public Utilities Commission with the power of pre-construction review and approval based upon these criteria. In 1970, the state of Washington established the first independent siting agency—the Thermal Power Plant Siting Evaluation Council—which was authorized to

---

11. The Administration bills were HR.10721, S.1934 (90th Congress). On the background of the legislation, see Federal Power Commission, *Prevention of Power Failures: Analyses and Recommendations.* (Washington, D.C., G.P.O. July 1967). On Congressional reaction, see *Congressional Quarterly 1967 Almanac,* p. 468 and *1969 Almanac,* pp. 537-538.

plan for future generating and transmission facility sites and to approve siting applications.[12]

Second, within the federal government, a major study conducted by the Office of Science and Technology and a committee of federal agency representatives and state regulatory commissioners stimulated a shift in emphasis toward the states. The major report of the study, *Electric Power and the Environment,* issued in 1970, stressed the following recommendation:

At present, preconstruction review of the expansion plans of the electric power industry at the state level are generally piecemeal, uncoordinated and incomplete. . . . (We) need an agency of government in each state or region empowered to review proposed alternatives and approve sites to assure compliance with land use and environmental protection standards before construction is scheduled to commence. The agency should have the authority to say "Yes, you are authorized to put it here" as well as to say, "No, don't put it there. . . ." The standard-setting machinery for air and water quality provides for enforcement at the state level. And, at present, decision-making authority on land use questions is also concentrated at the state level. Thus, in the absence of any federal jurisdiction, consolidating the authority for approvals of particular sites by the states appears appropriate.[13]

To provide the states with an incentive to act the committee also recommended that

Should an individual state or region fail to exercise the responsibility for certifying bulk power facilities to be built in that state or region, a federal agency to be designated by the President should assume the role until the state or regional agency assumes the job.[14]

In response to the committee's recommendation and the actions of the pioneering states, efforts to stimulate state action accelerated in 1970 and 1971.

In November 1970, the National Association of Regulatory Utility Commissioners, which worked closely with the federal committee, approved a widely publicized model statute which authorized a dominant state role in the siting of power plants and transmission lines. A number of other model siting statutes, such as that developed by the Council of State Governments, followed.

---

12. An informative analysis of the Washington experience may be found in Joseph McCarthy, "The Evolution of Washington Siting Legislation," 47 *Washington Law Review* 1 (1971).

13. Energy Policy Staff, Office of Science and Technology, *Electric Power and the Environment* (Washington, D.C., G.P.O., August 1970), p. 18.

14. Ibid., p. 9.

In March 1971, the Nixon administration submitted legislation to Congress which authorized a primary state role in coordinating power plant siting. The bill also authorized federal preemption in case of state failure to act. The proposed siting legislation received serious consideration in the 92nd Congress, and one bill (H.R. 11066) was eventually reported out to the House Interstate and Foreign Commerce Committee (although it failed to reach the floor). Similar legislation was considered in the 93rd and 94th Congresses.

By 1972, then, the agenda for innovation in power plant siting at the state level was firmly set. With national legislation encouraging state programs pending in Congress, with a number of model statutes in circulation, with several states having already passed new siting legislation, and with conflicts over nuclear plants growing ever more bitter, the need for legislative action by the remaining states seemed evident.

Large-Scale Developments

Concern over procedures for siting large-scale developments first became a prominent issue in 1970. In that year, Maine and Vermont both passed pioneering legislation which established a direct state role in the siting of facilities of major size and scope. In both cases, reform was precipitated by the perception of immediate and direct threats to the environment of the state.

In Vermont, uneasiness had existed for some time over land speculation and development by large out-of-state corporations. This uneasiness reached new proportions when the International Paper Company announced plans for a commercial and recreational development on 20,000 acres in southern Vermont. Several newspapers pointed out that most of the land was not covered by local planning, zoning, or subdivision controls. As a result, the governor appointed a Commission on Environmental Control to make a rapid study of the problem and prepare legislative recommendations. The commission's major conclusions, issued in late 1969, were that local planning, zoning, and subdivision controls could not be developed in time to regulate large-scale developments effectively and that, even if they could, the state had an obligation to plan and regulate the siting of such developments in the broader public interest.[15] The latter recommendation was implemented in Act 250, passed by the Vermont legislature in early 1970. The act established both a planning and regulatory framework for the siting of all major developments over ten acres in scope.

---

15. Discussions of the commission's work and the Vermont legislation are found in Bosselman and Callies, *The Quiet Revolution,* op. cit., pp. 54-88; Elizabeth Haskell and Victoria Price. *State Environmental Management* (New York, Praeger, 1973), pp. 169-191.

In Maine, a similar set of circumstances obtained. In 1969, the state was confronted with four large-scale proposals for deepwater ports and oil refineries along some of the most valued sections of its coastline. As in Vermont, few local governments in Maine exercised planning and regulatory powers over siting. Aroused by the outcry from conservation and citizen organizations, the governor appointed an Environmental Task Force which, with an eye on Vermont, proposed state regulation of siting. With certain modifications and exemptions (public utilities and residential developments), the Site Selection Law easily passed the 1970 legislature. The law subjected all industrial and commercial developments in excess of 20 acres to site review by the state Environmental Improvement Commission.[16]

The national impact of the Maine and Vermont innovations was considerably amplified by the Council on Environmental Quality's publication of *The Quiet Revolution in Land Use Control* in 1971. Bosselman and Callies described the Maine and Vermont initiatives in considerable detail and evaluated both experiments favorably. This report was one of the most significant documents in familiarizing planners, lawyers, and state officials with the concept of state control over siting.

By the time *The Quiet Revolution* appeared, debate was already underway over the national land use legislation proposals introduced by Senator Jackson of Washington and the Nixon administration.[17] In both proposals, regulation of large-scale developments by state government was a central feature. Jackson explained the rationale of his proposed act as follows:

One of the recurring and most complex problems of land use decision making today is that existing legal and institutional arrangements are in many respects archaic. They weren't designed to deal with contemporary problems. Industry, for example, is often unable to get effective decisions on plant siting and location without, in some cases, running the gauntlet of hearings, injunctions, and legal appeals. In other cases, however, under the banner of "broadening the tax base," industry is welcomed into areas which should be dedicated to other uses. Often this really means higher taxes, fewer amenities and more problems.

As public officials, we must find ways to accommodate new industrial expansion in harmony with other public values. We do not face an "either/or" proposition. It is not a question of industry or parks, jobs or natural beauty. It is a question of having the best of all of these. It is a question of having properly planned quality growth.

---

16. On the Maine experience, see Haskell and Price, *State Environmental Management,* op. cit., pp. 195-209.

17. The initial proposals were S.3354 (91st Congress), National Land Use Policy Act of 1970, introduced by Senator Jackson and S.992 (92nd Congres), National Land Use Policy Act of 1971, proposed by the Nixon administration. On the origin and evolution of these legislative proposals, see Noreen Lyday, *The Law of the Land* (Washington, D.C., The Urban Institute, 1976).

The land use policy bill I have proposed would require the establishment of industrial, conservation, and recreational sanctuaries. These sanctuaries would be established in advance of their need and on the basis of projected demands. Industrial sites would be located so that utility, transportation and environmental problems would be minimized.[18]

Congressional debate over the Jackson and Administration proposals continued through 1975. In all of the subsequent changes and amendments of the proposed legislation, the need for state-level control over large-scale developments has remained a fundamental component. It was perhaps the congressional debate more than any other factor that set the agenda for consideration of large-scale development siting reform in state legislatures.

A number of studies in the private sector also contributed significantly to encouraging reform of siting procedures for large-scale developments.

One important and influential proposal for siting reform was contained in the ALI Model Land Development Code. Articles 7 and 8 of the code envisioned the creation of a state plan and a State Land Adjudicatory Board which would exercise control over "developments of regional impact." The 1972 Florida Environmental Land and Water Management Act, which included state regulation of large-scale developments, was modeled directly on the ALI Code. The ALI Code was also the basis for revision of the proposed national land use legislation in the 92nd and 93rd Congresses.

The ABA's Special Committee on Environmental Law also began a major study of the siting problem during 1970 focusing upon the need

". . .to improve regulatory procedures, to reduce unnecessary multiplicity and overlap of regulatory regimes, and to establish some point of finality in the decision-making process all in a manner consistent with the broad social objectives of environmental quality."[19]

The Committee's report, issued in 1973, proposed the creation of an Industrial Siting Council (ISC) in each state with the power to preempt the decisionmaking authority of local jurisdictions and other state agencies with regard to all licenses, permits, and certifications for large-scale developments.[20] Just as the ALI draft articles, the special committee's legislative recommendations have had a direct impact. The Utah Industrial Facility

---

18. Senator Henry Jackson, Speech to the Washington State Association of Counties, June 1970. Printed in U.S. Congress, Senate, Committee on Interior and Insular Affairs, *National Land Use Policy Hearings on S.3354,* Part 2, 91st Congress, 2nd Session, July 8, 1970, p. 459.

19. Special Committee on Environmental Law, American Bar Association, *Industrial Development and the Environment,* op. cit., p. I-1.

20. Ibid., Chapter Three.

Siting Act, which narrowly missed passage in the 1975 legislature, was modeled directly on the committee's proposals.

Surface Mines

Regulation of surface mining for coal and other minerals has been a significant state legislative issue since the late thirties. West Virginia passed the first strip mining law in 1939, and thirty-one other states had passed similar laws as of December 1975. However, almost all of these statutes focus exclusively on reclamation of lands that have already been mined or are scheduled for mining. With varying degrees of stringency, these laws require submission of a reclamation plan to a state permitting agency, the posting of an insurance bond, and compliance with environmental standards for the conduct of mining operations so that reclamation can be effectively carried out. It is only in the last few years that the broader concept of advance planning and regulation of surface mine location has begun to receive extensive consideration.

The evolution of a positive approach to surface mine siting began in 1971 with the submission of a proposed Mined Area Protection Act to Congress by the Nixon administration.[21] Just as an earlier Johnson administration proposal in 1968, the 1971 bill sought to strengthen state regulatory programs through the imposition of federal standards for the reclamation and restoration of mined land. However, the 1971 version went beyond the earlier proposal in emphasizing the responsibility of the states to deny mining permits for land that could not, in each state's judgment, be adequately reclaimed for future use. This limited recognition of the need for siting control, which first appeared in the most advanced state statutes during the 1969-1970 period, still constituted an essentially passive and negative approach, resting on an extremely narrow conception of what land was unsuitable for mining. However, inclusion of the "unsuitability" concept in the Administration draft was extremely significant because it opened the door to further congressional elaboration and expansion of the advance siting approach.

Senate and House hearings on the Administration bill were held during 1971 and 1972; but like most of the President's environmental program, the Mined Area Protection Act was not given high priority in the Democratic Congress. It was not until after the 1972 election and resubmission of the Administration bill that serious legislative work got underway.

---

21. The text of the bill along with an explanation of the rationale for the legislation can be found in Council on Environmental Quality, *The President's 1971 Environmental Program* (Washington, D.C., G.P.O., 1971), pp. 271-288.

It was in congressional hearings during 1973 that a crucial broadening of the unsuitability concept took place.[22] In the Senate and House versions finally passed, the Administration's narrow conception of non-reclaimability was incorporated as a mandatory criterion of unsuitability. However, the legislation went far beyond the Administration bill to authorize state regulatory agencies to engage in wider planning, designation, and permitting processes. Specifically, the Surface Mining Control and Reclamation Act of 1974, Section 522(a), required the states to establish a "competent and scientifically sound" planning process on the basis of which

. . .a surface area may be designated unsuitable for certain types of surface coal mining operations if such operations will—

(A) be incompatible with existing land use plans or programs; or

(B) affect fragile or historic lands in which such operations could result in significant damage to important historic, cultural, scientific, and esthetic values and natural systems; or

(C) affect renewable resource lands in which such operations could result in a substantial loss or reduction of long-range productivity of water supply or of food or fiber products, and such lands to include aquifers and aquifer recharge areas; or

(D) affect natural hazard lands in which such operations could substantially endanger life and property, such lands to include areas subject to frequent flooding and areas of unstable geology.[23]

S. 425 thus established the framework for an aggressive, comprehensive state program of site planning and regulation.

Congressional creativity on S. 425 was stimulated by several factors. Senator Jackson and Representative Morris Udall of Arizona were the chief sponsors in their respective bodies of both S. 425 and the proposed National Land Use Policy Act. As a result, there was considerable cross-fertilization. The emphasis upon preserving fragile or historic lands, renewable resource lands, natural hazard lands, and aquifers and aquifer recharge lands found its way into the surface mine legislation as a direct reflection of the critical areas protection concept which formed the centerpiece of the general land use legislation. Indeed, the desire to coordinate the two legislative initiatives was explicit.[24] Second, there was strong pressure from organized environmental groups for some type of positive surface mining

---

22. See U.S. Congress, Senate, Committee on Interior and Insular Affairs, *Report on S.425, Surface Mining Reclamation Act of 1975,* 93rd Congress, First Session, September 21, 1973, pp. 67-69.

23. See U.S. Congress, Committee of Conference, *Report on S.425, Surface Mining Reclamation Act of 1974,* 93rd Congress, 2nd Session, December 5, 1974, pp. 51-52. See also the Conferee's explanation of the designation process, p. 78.

24. Section 522(a)(5) of S.425 notes that "Determinations of the unsuitability of land for surface coal mining, as provided in this section, shall be integrated as closely as possible with present and future land use planning and regulation processes at the Federal, State, and local levels."

control. In particular, the Coalition Against Strip Mining (which included most of the major environmental organizations) was a vigorous advocate of designation and site approval provisions. Finally, as corporate plans for extensive strip mining of western coal became evident during the oil crisis of 1973 and 1974, grazing and agricultural interests in the western states began to support more aggressive state programs in self-defense. Combined with growing Appalachian opposition to unfettered surface mining, this western constituency was a major influence in shaping an assertive approach to mine siting.

It should be noted that protection of the environment was not the only motivation for congressional authorization of positive siting procedures. As with reform in the siting of power plants and large-scale developments, the federal legislators also wanted to increase the certainty and finality of regulatory verdicts in order to expedite production of surface mined minerals. As the House Interior Committee noted:

The Committee believes that the area by area approach of Section 522 thus serves the industry since such a process may, in advance of application, identify lands which are either not open to surface mining or where surface mining is subject to restriction.[25]

Although both S. 425 and its successor (H. 25, 94th Congress) were vetoed by President Ford, the congressional debate has had an obvious effect at the state level. Most recent legislative proposals for siting reform are clearly based on the criteria, concepts, and arguments developed in the national legislation. The model statute on surface mine conservation and reclamation endorsed by the Council of State Governments in 1973 is also keyed to the proposed federal legislation.[26] The issue of surface mine siting control at the state level is still quite novel, but it is rapidly becoming a fixture on state legislative agendas.

POWER PLANT SITING LEGISLATION

Table III-1 presents the data on diffusion of power plant and transmission line siting legislation. The basic statute incorporates two elements of reform:

(1) It establishes a set of explicit policy criteria and/or a planning process for the identification of suitable and unsuitable power plant and transmission line sites.

(2) It authorizes a state regulatory agency to approve or disapprove the use of particular sites on the basis of those criteria and/or plans.

25. U.S. Congress, House, Committee on Interior and Insular Affairs, Report on HR.25, *Surface Mining Control and Reclamation Act of 1975*, 94th Congress, 1st Session, March 6, 1975, p. 91. Note: HR.25 is identical to S.425 in the 93rd Congress.

26. Council on State Governments, *Suggested State Legislation 1974* (Lexington, Kentucky, The Council, 1973), pp. 22-35 (Surface Mining Conservation and Reclamation Act).

TABLE—III-1

DIFFUSION OF POWER PLANT SITING LEGISLATION
(As of December 1975)

State	Year	Statute
Vermont	1969	Vt. S.A., Title 30, Section 248
Washington State	1970	R.C.W., Section 80.50.010 to 80.50.900
South Carolina	1971	S.C. Gen. and Perm. Laws, Section 58-1801 to 58-1831
Maryland	1971	Maryland Power Plant Siting Act of 1971, Md. C.A., Section 3-301 to 3-307
Nevada	1971	Utility Environmental Protection Act. Nev. R.S., Section 704.820 to 704.900
Arizona	1971	A.R.S., Section 40-360 to 40-360.12
Connecticut	1971	Public Utility Environmental Standards Act. Conn. Gen. Stat., Section 16-50h to 16-50y
New Mexico	1971	N.M.S.A., Section 68-7-1 to 68-7-4
Oregon	1971	O.R.S., Section 469.300 to 469.992
New Hampshire	1971	N.H.R.S.A., Section 162-F:1 to 162-F:13
New York	1972	Siting of Major Steam Electric Generating Facilities Act, McKinney's Consolidated Laws of N.Y., Public Service Law, Article 8, Section 140 to 149b.
Ohio	1972	Ohio Rev. Code. Ann. Section 4906.01 to 4906.99
Montana	1973	Montana Major Facility Siting Act, R.C. of Mont., Section 70-801 to 70-829
Florida	1973	The Florida Electrical Power Plant Siting Act, F.S.A., Section 403.501 to 403.515
Arkansas	1973	The Utility Facility Environmental Protection Act, Ark. S.A., Section 73-276.1 to 73-276.18
Minnesota	1973	Minnesota Power Plant Siting Act. M.S.A. Section 116C.51 to 116C.69
California	1974	Cal. Public Resources Code, Section 25500 to 25542
Kentucky	1974	The Power Plant Siting Act of 1974, H.B. 438, 1974 Reg. Sess.
Massachusetts	1974	Ann. Laws of Mass., Chapter 164, Section 69K to 69R
North Dakota	1975	North Dakota Energy Conversion and Transmission Facility Siting Act. N.D. Century Code, Section 49-22-01 to 49-22-23
Wyoming	1975	Wyo. S.A., Section 35.502.75 to 35.502.94
Wisconsin	1975	Ch. 68, Laws of 1975

(Continued)

TABLE III-1 (Continued)

Proposed Legislation[1]

Texas (Defeated by House, 1974)
New Jersey (Defeated by House, 1974)
Pennsylvania (Passed by Senate, Defeated by House, 1974)

---

1. Reported out favorably to a full chamber during last two sessions.

The most striking feature of Table III-1 is the absence of legislative leadership by either the large, affluent, urbanized states or by any particular region. Vermont and Washington were the originators of siting legislation in 1969 and 1970 respectively. They were followed in 1971 by eight states distributed throughout the nation. This pattern of widely dispersed adoptions has been followed in subsequent years. The only significant variation in receptivity in the period since first adoption is that the Northeast and West have been somewhat quicker to embrace the innovation than the South and Midwest. Eight western and seven northeastern states had adopted a statute by December 1975, in contrast to three midwestern and four southern states.

In all, twenty-two states have accepted the innovation in just six years. This diffusion rate is among the fastest for any legislative innovation in recent American history. Although the number of adoptions per year has not accelerated in the past few legislative sessions, the average number of enactments per year three to four remains high.

This rapid diffusion of power plant and transmission line siting legislation has been due to several factors. First, the threat of federal preemption incorporated in the legislation considered by Congress during the past four years has given the states a strong incentive to act before being forced to.

Second, the issue has been thoroughly "professionalized," receiving the endorsements of organizations ranging from the National Association of Regulatory Utility Commissioners to the Association of the Bar of New York City to the Council of State Governments. These endorsements have made it much easier to garner legislative support, because the legislation can be portrayed as a nonpolitical effort to modernize state government in accordance with standard professional practice.

Diffusion of the legislation has also been speeded by the fact that innovation is essentially incremental. Many state Public Service and Public Utility Commissions have been issuing certificates of "public convenience and necessity" for the construction of power plants and transmission lines

45

for years. This procedure, which focuses on the relationship of the proposed plant to future service reliability, already involves an elaborate pre-construction review. The addition of environmental and land use considerations to the existing procedure does not constitute a radical departure from existing practice. Of course, many of the states have established entirely new siting agencies, mandated the consolidation of all environmental permit procedures, preempted local control, and so forth. However, the fact that legislatures can embrace the essence of the innovation without making a radical departure or setting up a new agency has clearly speeded diffusion.

Finally, political opposition to power plant and transmission line siting legislation has been minimal. Electric utility companies, with some exceptions, support a stronger state role, and some, as mentioned earlier, have even solicited the development of state programs. Environmental and community groups, also with some exceptions, have favored the innovation. Although some environmentalists believe that power plant and transmission lines regulation ought to be a component of a broader state land use planning and management program instead of being included in narrow-purpose siting legislation, environmental opposition has not been strong enough to preclude passage of a state-level siting statute in any legislature where the innovation has been seriously considered.

LARGE-SCALE DEVELOPMENT SITING LEGISLATION

Table III-2 presents data on the diffusion of large-scale development siting legislation. The core elements of the innovation are two:

(1) The statute establishes a set of policy criteria and/or a planning process to identify desirable and undesirable areas for large-scale development.

(2) The statute vests a state regulatory agency with the power to enforce the criteria and/or plans through review and permitting of site applications.

There is a strong pattern of regional variation in receptivity. Of the six states that enacted the innovation as of December 1975, four were in the Northeast. Defining region in another way, five of the six were eastern seaboard states. What these states have in common is extremely heavy pressure for industrial and commercial development in their coastal zone and shoreland areas. It should be noted that two of the more recent enactments, in Delaware and New Jersey, limit state-level control of large-scale development to projects on coastal land. Legislative activity in the Northeast has continued to be vigorous. The New Hampshire legislature narrowly missed passage of a comprehensive statute in 1975 and the Maryland legislature enacted an energy facilities siting act in 1975.

Outside the eastern seaboard, only Wyoming has enacted an innovative siting law. However, Wyoming's action seems to be the forerunner of

TABLE III-2

DIFFUSION OF LARGE-SCALE DEVELOPMENT SITING LEGISLATION
(As of December 1975)

State	Year of Adoption	Statute
Maine	1970**	Site Location of Development Act, Me. R.S.A., Title 38, Section 481 to 489
Vermont	1970**	Vt. S.A., Title 10, Section 6001 to 6089
Delaware	1971*	Delaware Coastal Zone Act. Del. C.A., Section 7-7001 to 7-7013
Florida	1972**	Florida Environmental Land and Water Management Act of 1972, F.S.A., Section 380.012 to 380.10
New Jersey	1973*	Coastal Area Facility Review Act: N.J.S.A., Section 13:19-1 to 13:19-21
Wyoming	1975**	Industrial Development Information and Siting Act. Wyom. S.A., Section 35-502.75 to 35.502.94

Proposed Legislation[1]

Wisconsin (Defeated by House, 1974)
Idaho (Defeated by Senate, 1975)
New Hampshire (Defeated by House, 1975)
Utah (Defeated by House, 1975)
Iowa (Passed by House, tabled by Senate, 1975)

*Coastal Areas Only
**Entire State

1. Reported out to a full chamber during last two sessions.

extensive legislative activity among the western states. During 1975, large-scale development siting statutes came very close to approval in the Idaho and Utah legislatures. Montana and North Dakota passed legislation during 1975 providing state-level control over the siting of large-scale energy conversion and development facilities. These initiatives form a favorable base from which to consider more inclusive siting legislation. All of the western states undertaking legislative activity are reacting to the same phenomenon—the initiation of rapid industrial development due to the possession of large, exploitable energy reserves.

A striking feature of Table III-2 is the absence of legislative leadership by the larger, wealthier, and more industrialized states that have traditionally taken the lead in innovation, such as California in the West, New York and Massachusetts in the Northeast, and Michigan in the Midwest. Indeed, most of the innovators in the Northeast and West are rural and agricultural states with small dispersed populations. To some degree, these states reflect special conditions, such as the energy-related development pressure which confronted Maine in 1970 and affects Wyoming today. But the disinterest of the larger states also seems to reflect more basic factors, such as the shift in industrial growth away from the older populous states as well as stronger traditions of sophisticated industrial siting and development control at the local level.

The diffusion rate for large-scale development siting legislation has been average—six adoptions over a five-year span. Legislative activity has been consistent, with at least one enactment or vote in a full chamber in every year except 1971. The amount of legislative activity (apart from actual enactments) picked up substantially during 1975.

One of the major reasons why large-scale siting legislation has not diffused more rapidly—i.e., on the order of power plant siting legislation—is the cost. Legislatures have not been willing to place siting authority in economic development departments; so most have set up new bureaucratic agencies or greatly expanded state planning offices. Mandatory application fees partially offset the expense of operating a siting program, but the cost of setting up and maintaining a new agency that is not eligible for direct federal subsidy constitutes a significant roadblock to favorable action on the innovation. Thus, the failure of national land use legislation has directly affected the diffusion of siting legislation.

SURFACE MINE SITING LEGISLATION

Dates of adoption of surface mine siting legislation are presented in Table III-3. The typical innovative statute incorporates two essential features:

1. It establishes policy criteria and/or a planning process for the designation of land areas which are suitable and unsuitable for surface mining.
2. It authorizes a state agency to deny mining permits on lands which are deemed unsuitable.

Two of the enacted statutes provide for preemption of local controls and consolidation of environmental review. The others do not.

Surface mine siting legislation is widely dispersed, but one focus of regional receptiveness based on common problems has appeared. Montana forms a northern Great Plains cluster with the two midwestern adop-

TABLE III-3

DIFFUSION OF SURFACE MINE SITING LEGISLATION
(As of December 1975)

State	Year of Adoption	Statute
Montana	1973	The Montana Strip Mining and Reclamation Act, R.C.M., Section 50-1034 to 50-1057
California	1975	The Surface Mining and Reclamation Act of 1975, California Public Resources Code, Section 2710 to 2793
North Dakota	1975	North Dakota Century Code. Section 38-14-01 to 38-14-12
South Dakota	1975	South Dakota Compiled Laws, Section 45-6A-2 to 45-6A-31
Texas	1975	Texas Surface Mining and Reclamation Act, Vernon's Texas Annotated Civil Statutes, Article 5290-10, Section 1-27

ters, South and North Dakota. These are among the states facing the greatest pressure for surface coal mining in the 1970s. Texas—the lone southern adopter—and California appear to have acted in response to accelerated demand for other types of surface-mined minerals such as phosphates and clays. As yet, the innovation has not been seriously considered in the larger states of the Northeast and Midwest which have traditionally enacted the strictest surface mining reclamation statutes—Pennsylvania, Ohio, and Illinois—or in the states with the worst strip mining abuses—Kentucky and West Virginia.

The rate of diffusion has been quite rapid, five states in three years. If this pace is maintained, the legislation may rival power plant siting legislation as one of the most quickly adopted innovations in recent history. Just as power plant siting, state level regulation of surface mine siting enjoys the advantage of "incrementalism." State agencies for the control of surface mines are already operating in most states with minerals subject to surface extraction, and new responsibilities can be added without the expense of establishing a new regulatory bureaucracy. Surface mining reform also has benefited from the extensive national attention devoted to the need for exploiting our vast coal reserves. Environmental reaction to coal company plans, as incorporated in the proposed federal legislation, has raised the issue of proper siting of surface mines to a prominent plateau.

CONCLUSION

Of the three types of siting legislation discussed in this chapter—power plant and transmission lines, large-scale industrial and commerical developments, and surface mines—only the second shows a marked regional focus. As Table III-4 indicates, legislation regulating the siting of large-scale developments has been confined to the eastern seaboard, with the exception of Wyoming. Legislation regulating the siting of power plants and transmission lines, and of surface mines, on the other hand, has been fairly well-dispersed throughout the nation.

Of the three types of legislation, power plant and transmission line siting reform has been the most acceptable innovation. Twenty-two states

TABLE III-4

SUMMARY STATISTICS:
DIFFUSION OF SITING LEGISLATION

ADOPTION INFORMATION	TYPE OF LEGISLATION		
	Power Plants and Transmission Lines	Large-Scale Industrial and Commercial Developments	Surface Mines
Date of First Adoption	1970	1970	1973
Total Number of Adoptions	22	6	5
Most Adoptions in One Year	8 (1971)	2 (1970)	4 (1975)
Adoptions by Region			
Northeast	7	4	0
South	4	1	1
Midwest	3	0	2
West	8	1	2

have adopted this type of legislation within six years. However there was extensive legislative activity on large-scale development siting during 1974 and 1975, (although the legislation was defeated or tabled in five states) and surface mine siting adoptions accelerated during 1975.

Table III-5 shows the time interval, in years, between the adoption by the first state (designated by 0) and adoption by other states for each type of statute. Vermont is the only state which can legitimately be termed a national legislative leader. Within the other regions, pioneering states in siting reform are evident: Florida in the South, Montana in the West, North Dakota in the Midwest.

The most striking feature is the absence of expected leadership by the more affluent, industrialized, and populous states that normally play in the "national league" of competition for legislative preeminence. Instead, innovation in siting reform has been led primarily by smaller rural, developing states. We have attributed this to three factors:

1. The pressures of industrial and commercial development have slackened in the larger states of the Northeast and Midwest and accelerated in the smaller states over the past decade.

2. Local land use and economic development agencies tend to be more sophisticated in the larger, more affluent states, thus lessening the incentive for state-level reform.

3. The less populated and less industrialized states, of the West and Southwest in particular, have stronger traditions of state government and lesser concentrations of urban resistance than the larger states.

TABLE III-5

SUMMARY STATISTICS: STATE ACTION ON SITING LEGISLATION
(Time Interval Since First Adoption, in Years)

State	Power Plants and Transmission Lines	Large-Scale Industrial and Commercial Developments	Surface Mines
Alabama	—	—	—
Alaska	—	—	—
Arizona	2	—	—
Arkansas	4	—	—
California	5	—	2
Colorado	—	—	—
Connecticut	2	—	—
Delaware	—	2	—
Florida	4	2	—

(Continued)

51

TABLE III-5 (Continued)

State	Power Plants and Transmission Lines	Large-Scale Industrial and Commercial Developments	Surface Mines
Georgia	—	—	—
Hawaii	—	—	—
Idaho	—	—	—
Illinois	—	—	—
Indiana	—	—	—
Iowa	—	—	—
Kansas	—	—	—
Kentucky	5	—	—
Louisiana	—	—	—
Maine	—	0	—
Maryland	2	—	—
Massachusetts	5	—	—
Michigan	—	—	—
Minnesota	5	—	—
Mississippi	—	—	—
Missouri	—	—	—
Montana	4	—	0
Nebraska	—	—	—
Nevada	2	—	—
New Hampshire	2	—	—
New Jersey	—	3	—
New Mexico	2	—	—
New York	3	—	—
North Carolina	—	—	—
North Dakota	6	—	2
Ohio	3	—	—
Oklahoma	—	—	—
Oregon	2	—	—
Pennsylvania	—	—	—
Rhode Island	—	—	—
South Carolina	2	—	—
South Dakota	—	—	2
Tennessee	—	—	—
Texas	—	—	2
Utah	—	—	—
Vermont	0	0	—
Virginia	—	—	—
Washington	1	—	—
West Virginia	—	—	—
Wisconsin	6	—	—
Wyoming	6	5	—

IV. NATURAL AREAS LEGISLATION

This chapter examines the spread of innovative statutes which establish state-level controls upon land development in designated natural areas. Protection of unique or unusually valuable land through state-level regulation is perhaps the most controversial innovation in land use governance. The controversy is due both to legal uncertainty over the limits of state police power and to the acute sensitivity of local governments to potential tax losses from state-imposed restrictions upon growth. Nevertheless, a significant number of state legislatures have already enacted statutes to protect natural areas.

Three types of natural areas protection legislation will be examined in detail:

1. Wetlands protection statutes;
2. Shorelands protection statutes; and
3. Critical environmental areas protection statutes.

As in previous chapters, it should be emphasized that the specific intergovernmental relationships authorized by such statutes differ widely from state to state, and reference to a state's adoption of one of these types of legislation does not connote any similarity in the specific responsibilities assigned to state and local government.

THE RATIONALE FOR PROTECTION

The need for restriction of development in natural areas became a significant focus of reform efforts in the mid-sixties when a number of major constituencies—old-line conservation groups, emerging environmental associations, sportsmen's clubs and scientific organizations—began to criticize the rapid pace of residential, commercial, and industrial development which local governments were allowing in areas of fragile and unstable ecology. From their perspective, development in those areas seriously threatened human health and safety, the preservation of animal species, and many of the recreational and aesthetic values which were of increasing importance to a crowded urban society.

Natural areas such as woodlands, shorelands, deserts, mountains, and wetlands have, of course, traditionally attracted residential development because of their aesthetic attractions and recreational opportunities. Shorelands, wetlands, and estuaries have also attracted agriculture, industry, and commerce because of the convenience of water-borne transportation or the relatively low land costs. Prior to the sixties, development in these natural areas did not arouse great concern except among some traditional conservation groups. The amount of available land across the nation seemed so vast and the rate of development moderate enough that few devoted much attention to the consequences of exploitation. Indeed, for example, a number of states actually encouraged the draining of wetlands for agricultural use. The federal government protected some natural areas through acquisition under the various national park, national forest, and wildlife conservation acts, and the states enjoyed their own park programs; but most natural areas remained unprotected, except where local governments imposed regulatory controls under general state planning, zoning, and subdivision enabling statutes. Because most natural areas were located in rural jurisdictions which had no planning or zoning apparatus to start with, the coverage of regulatory protection was slight. In those areas with controls, most local politicians enjoyed neither the desire nor the public support to pursue a strategy of natural areas protection, because development on previously "unusable" lands such as wetlands and deserts brought in vitally needed property tax revenues.

Laissez faire attitudes toward natural areas began to change in the sixties as a result of the staggering scope and pace of development from the mid-fifties onward. For example, twenty-nine percent of the coastal wetlands on Long Island were bulkheaded and filled for residential development between 1955 and 1964.[1] On the other side of the continent, industrial and commercial developers filled more than 240 square miles of San Francisco Bay through 1965.[2] In southern Florida, tens of thousands of acres of ecologically sensitive swampland were developed to accommodate Dade County's growing population.[3] In the northern lake country of Wisconsin, Minnesota, and Michigan, most of the available shoreline was sold for second-home development from 1955 to 1965 as the new interstate highways made automobile travel quicker and easier.[4] Issues such as the Everglades Jetport conflict, the Machiasport oil refinery proposal, and the Storm King Mountain power plant controversy helped crystalize the notion that the nation's natural areas were under siege from rapacious and ecologically insensitive developers.

---

1. Ralph Green, *Wetlands on Long Island* (Hauppauge, N.Y., Nassau-Suffolk Regional Planning Board, 1972). For a more detailed study, see also J.S. O'Connor and O.W. Terry, *The Marine Wetlands of Nassau and Suffolk Counties, New York* (Hauppauge, N.Y., Nassau-Suffolk Regional Planning Board, 1972).

2. Note, "San Francisco Bay: Regional Regulation For its Protection and Development," 55 *California Law Review* 728 (1967).

3. Luther J. Carter, *The Florida Experience: Land and Water Policy in a Growth State* (Baltimore, Johns Hopkins University Press, 1974), Chapters 3-7.

4. Douglas Yanggen and Jon Kusler, "Natural Resources Protection Through Shoreland Regulation: Wisconsin," 44 *Land Economics* 73 (1968).

The concerns generated by rapid development in natural areas fell into four major categories.

First, and perhaps of greatest importance, there was concern over the impact of rapid and unplanned development upon water supply and quality. One issue of prime significance was the drainage and filling of wetlands. By the mid-1960s, scientific evidence established the crucial role of swamps, marshes, bogs, and fens as buffer zones for the absorption and retention of floodwaters.[5] Maintenance of such natural buffer areas is important not only to prevent flooding of surrounding areas but also to replenish underground aquifers. Protection of wetlands assumed particular importance in such states as Florida and Wisconsin, which depend heavily upon aquifers for fresh water.

The degradation of the nation's major estuaries also aroused heavy criticism. The quality of water in such estuaries as Delaware Bay, Puget Sound, Narragansett Bay, and San Francisco Bay declined significantly between 1955 and 1965 as rapidly expanding industrial enterprises with shoreline locations discharged their wastes into public waters. Degradation of the estuarine environment created very serious problems for commercial fishermen as well as other users of the water.

Another water-related issue was the impact of unplanned residential development along lakeshores and streams in degrading water quality through septic-tank runoff and erosion. This concern initially arose in Wisconsin, Michigan, and Minnesota, where second-home development had boomed along northern lakeshores. As water quality declined, doubt was aroused concerning the future of the economically vital recreation industry.[6]

Second, rapid and poorly planned development in natural areas also generated direct threats to public health and safety. Perhaps the most significant of these was the susceptibility of many second-home and recreational developments to flooding. In rural areas lacking land use controls, developers often constructed second homes immediately adjacent to rivers, streams, and lakes or on newly drained and filled wetlands. These homes inevitably were damaged by floods. A related issue was the susceptibility of much construction in shore areas to damage from erosion. This problem was particularly evident along the Great Lakes and the Pacific

---

5. For a brief summary on scientific evidence on the ecological importance of inland wetlands, see Christa Schwintzer, "Wetlands and Why They Are Important," *Lakeland Report* (University of Michigan Biological Station Newsletter), August 1975. On coastal wetlands, see John Clark, *Coastal Ecosystems* (Washington, D.C., The Conservation Foundation, 1974).

6. See Yanggen and Kusler, "Natural Resource Protection," op. cit., p. 75-76.

Coast. One government report estimated erosion damage to private property along the Lake Michigan shoreline at $20 million to $50 million during 1968-1969.[7]

Concern about public safety was also aroused by extensive second-home and recreational development in mountainous areas in such states as Colorado, Idaho, New Hampshire, and Vermont. Much of this development took place on steep slopes naturally susceptible to landslides, rockslides, and other forms of erosion.[8] Grading and destruction of ground cover often compounded the problem.

Third, the rapid and extensive land development of the fifties and sixties aroused concern about the destruction of public recreational rights and opportunities. One focus of attention was the draining and filling of wetlands, an American tradition ever since the late eighteenth century. As vacant land—particularly vacant land near major cities—became scarcer in the fifties and sixties, developers were attracted to wetlands because of their low cost. At the same time local governments were pleased to have "unproductive" land added to the tax rolls.

Meanwhile, however, in contrast to previous indifferent attitudes, sportsmen and conservationists began to emphasize the value of wetlands as havens for pursuits such as hiking, boating, fishing, hunting, bird-watching, and photography. The U.S. Water Resources Council noted that

It was only recently realized that undisturbed marshes, swamps and overflow lands have a variety of aesthetic, environmental, and recreational values and a significant complex relation to their biotic communities. . . . The value of many wetlands in their natural state lies in the commercial and recreational value of the fish and wildlife they support. Most species of waterfowl and many fur animals are totally dependent upon wetland environments for their survival and well-being. Many marine, estuarine, and freshwater fishes of sport and commercial importance also depend upon wetlands during part or all of their lives. As these creatures become less abundant, modern man often places a higher value on them, and wetlands become worth more than anything he can put in their place.[9]

Another recreational issue involved public access to beaches. As increased amounts of oceanfront and lakefront land were privately developed, the general public was gradually excluded from beach recreation

---

7. U.S. Congress, House of Representatives, Subcommittee on Rivers and Harbors, *Shoreline Protection, Hearing on H.R. 12712,* 91st Congress, 1st Session, November 20, 1969, p. 8.

8. See Donald Nichols and Catherine Campbell (eds.), *Environmental Planning and Geology* (Washington, D.C., G.P.O., 1971). For a more popular treatment of steep slope hazards, see Ian McHarg, *Design With Nature* (Garden City, N.Y., Natural History Press, 1971).

9. United States Water Resources Council, *The Nation's Water Resources* (Washington, D.C., G.P.O., 1968), pp. 5-7-1, 5-7-2.

outside of parks and preserves. Exclusion of the public—often accomplished in a punitive and insulting manner—was allowed even though almost all the states asserted ownership in public trust to all submerged lands and beach areas up to the high-water mark.[10] Controversy over beach access assumed particular significance in such states as California, Massachusetts, and Florida, where beaches are widely used for mass recreation.

Attention also was drawn to the effects of water pollutants from industrial complexes, power plants, and public facilities on fishing, recreation, and aesthetic enjoyment in the nation's estuaries and Great Lakes. By the mid-sixties, heated conflicts between recreational and industrial users of the estuarine environment were common across the country, and skepticism about the value of continued industrial and commercial expansion along the shoreline was clearly evident. As the final report of the National Estuarine Pollution Study noted,

It is the value of the estuarine zone as a fish and wildlife habitat, a recreational resource, and an aesthetic attraction that makes the estuarine zone a unique feature of the human environment, yet it is these very values that have been generally ignored in satisfying the immediate social and economic needs of civilization. . . . The values of the estuarine zone as a fish and wildlife habitat, as a recreational facility, and as an aesthetic experience are probably greater than they are for commercial exploitation. . . .[11]

Of course, most critics recognized that some industrial and commercial expansion should and would continue, but they made a strong case for the need to impose a comprehensive process of public planning and control of estuarine use upon the haphazard workings of the private market.

The final set of concerns voiced by critics of development involved the diminution of diversity in the natural environment. From the perspective of many scientists, conservationists, and other interested citizens, extensive development in natural areas posed a serious threat to one of the most important values of all; maintenance of the full natural diversity of animal and plant species and ecosystems. Certainly, no one claimed that every natural area represented a critical resource for species preservation. However, in the aggregate, the rapid exploitation of virgin natural areas cast serious doubt upon the ability of nature to sustain the full array of flora and fauna native to the United States.

---

10. See Joseph Sax, "The Public Trust Doctrine in Natural Resource Law: Effective Judicial Intervention" 68 *Michigan Law Review* 473 (1970); Note, "The Public Trust in Tidal Areas: A Sometimes Submerged Traditional Doctrine" 79 *Yale Law Journal* 762 (1970).

11. U.S. Congress, *The National Estuarine Pollution Study*, Report Submitted by the Secretary of Interior Pursuant to P.L. 89-753, 92nd Congress, 2nd Session, March 25, 1970, p. 40.

Perhaps the principal argument for diversity was that a broad-based genetic pool is essential to the survival and adaptive capacity of all plant and animal life, including man. As a report of the Council on Environmental Quality noted,

Man depends directly on thousands of species of living organisms for his needs and indirectly on the adaptive diversity and ecological roles played by countless others. Although the apparent importance of some of these species to man may be aesthetic or of human interest, it is well known, albeit frequently not well understood, that each kind of living organism occupies a particular role or niche in the environment and that the survival of sufficient numbers of individuals of any species may be important to the dynamic functioning of the total ecosystems in which they occur.[12]

It has been estimated that among the higher vertebrate species alone, more than fifty have been extinguished due to human activity in the United States.[13] Many more continue to be seriously threatened. Although special refuges provide protection for some endangered species, many scientists and conservationists question whether the refuges alone assure diversity. One article contained this gloomy forecast:

The day is rapidly approaching when the remnants of the natural environment will be contained in a patchwork of parks and preserves. Much of the world's biological endowment will then be locked into insular refugia that are surrounded by inhospitable landscape, through which dispersal to the next refuge is slow or nonexistent.[14]

A second argument for the maintenance of diversity relates to the advancement of scientific knowledge. Disciplines ranging from botany and zoology to archaeology and anthropology depend on natural areas for research and educational instruction. A sufficient reserve of representative natural areas is essential to the progress of scientific investigation in these fields, which in turn are often the key to successful advancement of human enterprises in agriculture, industry, and so forth. Thus, many scientists maintained, there should be a careful public balancing of scientific needs versus development plans in deciding on the use of natural areas.[15]

The final argument for preservation and protection is that human beings impoverish their own existence by limiting the diversity of their con-

12. Council on Environmental Quality, *Fifth Annual Report* (Washington, D.C., G.P.O., December, 1974), pp. 325-326.

13. Ibid., p. 324.

14. John Terborgh, "Preservation of Natural Diversity: The Problem of Extinction Prone Species," 24 *Bioscience* 715 (1974), p. 715.

15. The Nature Conservancy, *The Preservation of Natural Diversity: A Survey and Recommendations* (Washington, D.C., The Conservancy, 1975); Rezneat Darnell, *Ecology and Man* (Dubuque, Iowa, W.C. Brown Co., 1973).

tacts with nature. The change and challenge of contact with a diverse natural environment provides an aesthetic and spiritual uplift for people, particularly for the large proportion of the population that lives in urban areas. Of course, parks provide part of the answer to the problem. However, most parks are oriented to mass recreation rather than preservation of the environment, and it is the rare jurisdiction that has sufficient funds for park acquisition to keep pace with the rapid rate of development. Thus, a broader strategy of insuring diversity was required.

THE ACQUISITION STRATEGY

Acquisition is the traditional means of protecting valuable land resources in the United States. Indeed, public purchase of either fee simple title or development rights to natural areas has been the major rallying cry of American conservationists since the founding of the movement more than seventy-five years ago. Gifford Pinchot, Aldo Leopold, John Muir, and others all stressed acquisition as the only means of conclusively and permanently protecting natural areas. Regulation might be less costly, conservationists admitted, but it was too subject to manipulation, corruption, and legal challenge by profit-oriented private landowners. Once land was publicly acquired, no compromises with private interests had to be made.

Given the strength and longevity of this tradition, it is not surprising that one major response to the concerns generated by the inadequacies and insensitivity of local regulation was support for accelerated acquisition programs at all levels of government. Conservationists, environmentalists, sportsmen, scientists, and other concerned constituencies achieved extraordinary success from the mid-1960s onward. New federal legislation established the National Wildlife Refuge System (P.L. 89-669, 1966), the National Wild and Scenic Rivers System (P.L. 90-542, 1968), the Endangered Species Conservation program (P.L. 91-135, 1970), and the Water Bank program (P.L. 91-559, 1971). Most significant of all was the Land and Water Conservation Act of 1965, (P.L. 88-578) which authorized up to $200 million per year for acquisition of parks, wildlife refuges, scenic areas, historic sites, and recreation areas by federal conservation agencies and by state and local governments.

Significant progress was also achieved at the state level. Between 1962 and 1970, state park agencies increased their expenditures for land acquisition from less than $20 million to more than $75 million per year.[16] Part of this increase was derived from Land and Water Conservation Fund

---

16. *State Park Statistics* (Washington, D.C., National Recreation and Parks Association, 1970).

money, but most of it represented increased spending by the states themselves, derived either from publicly approved bond issues or general appropriations. Under the prodding of concerned constituencies, a number of states also introduced more aggressive policies for protecting and preserving natural areas on lands they already owned or planned to acquire. In 1965, for example, Oregon designated the entire state-owned shoreline between the high- and low-water marks as a public recreation area and aggressively enforced public rights against the encroachments of private landowners. In 1967, the state of Washington designated its entire seashore as a conservation area and established protective use guidelines. Beginning in the late fifties, many states initiated or strengthened programs for the designation and protection of special natural areas within state-owned parks and forest lands.

There was also a significant upsurge of acquisition at the local level in the sixties. Perhaps the foremost manifestation of local efforts to protect natural areas was the authorization and formation of special conservation commissions in the northeastern states. Initiated by Massachusetts in 1957, conservation commissions are official local bodies charged with responsibility for protecting the natural environment through the acquisition and management of open space and critical habitats. By 1970, conservation commissions were operating in seven northeastern states. Particularly in Connecticut and Massachusetts, the commissions were highly successful in tapping state and federal acquisition funds as well as in stimulating local bond issues.[17]

Despite the success of efforts to expand land acquisition, many concerned citizens and government officials doubted whether purchase alone could provide an adequate or appropriate response to the problems posed by rapid development. The major source of skepticism was the obvious imbalance between available (or potentially available) funding and the amount of land that would have to be acquired. Even with total funding levels of more than $300 million per year, federal, state, and local acquisition programs could hardly hope to purchase more than a small fraction of the areas which required protection. Steeply escalating land costs exacerbated this imbalance and discouraged total reliance on acquisition. At best, it was realized, acquisition could preserve and protect only those sites of greatest natural value.

There was also a feeling among several of the concerned constituencies—planners and lawyers in particular—that purchase was not always necessary to protect the values inherent in the natural environment. Why,

---

17. Charles Morrison Jr., "Local Environmental Conservation Commissions: The Beginning of a National Movement," *Outdoor Recreation Action,* Report No. 29, Fall 1973.

for example, acquire and manage a wetland when the goal of maintaining water flow and protecting wildlife could be attained by requiring private structures to be constructed on poles? Why acquire a shoreland area when landowners could be required to provide public access to the beach? Protective regulations might thus accomplish many conservation goals at much less cost than acquisition. At the same time, private citizens could continue to enjoy the pleasures and prerogatives of landownership in natural areas which were so obviously desired by large proportions of the population. Of course, acquisition would still be required where protective regulation could not successfully accomplish conservation goals or in cases of successful legal challenge, but to many it made sense both practically and theoretically to rely on regulation as a first line of defense against destructive development.

THE ORIGINS OF STATE PROTECTIVE LEGISLATION

As an alternative to acquisition, the second major response to rapid land development was thus an effort to stimulate more aggressive and ecologically sensitive *regulation* under the police power. By a process of elimination, attention rapidly centered on the pivotal role of state government in carrying out this function.

Federal regulation of development in natural areas was limited to the exercise of permit authority by the Army Corps of Engineers over dredging, filling, and dumping in navigable waters under the Rivers and Harbors Act of 1899. In 1958, Congress enacted the Fish and Wildlife Coordination Act, which required the Corps to give consideration to protection of natural habitats for flora and fauna in the permit process. It was not until 1967, however, at the prodding of conservationists, scientists, and sportsmen, that the Corps and the U.S. Fish and Wildlife Service reached an agreement for systematic consultation with each other. Even at this point, the Corps was not anxious to use its regulatory authority for anything other than the protection of navigability. It took the landmark case of *Zabel* v. *Tabb* (1970) in the federal courts to persuade the Corps that it had a responsibility to take fish and wildlife protection seriously.[18]

Beyond the Corp's reticence to take preservation to heart, it was also recognized that the permitting program was of limited significance relative

---

18. *Zabel v. Tabb,* 430 F. 2d 199 (August, 1970). Even after the Zabel case, the protection of wetlands and wildlife habitats afforded by the Corps program remains questionable. Under existing constraints of manpower and funding, it has been impossible for the Corps and the Fish and Wildlife Service to give careful consideration to more than a fraction of the dredge, fill, and discharge requests they receive. One article indicates that over half of permit requests are handled with "no action" reports by the Fish and Wildlife Service, indicating that no analysis of the need for protection has been undertaken. See "The Wetlands: How Well Are They Protected," *Conservation Foundation Letter,* September 1974.

to the overall problems posed by rapid development in the nation's natural areas, because it only covered areas in and around navigable waters, an important but narrow segment of the natural areas that required protection if meaningful conservation goals were to be attained.[19] Given the limitations of the federal permit power, advocates of more aggressive regulation naturally looked to the police power authority over land use vested in state government. The states, of course, had long ago delegated that authority over land use to local governments under planning, zoning, and subdivision enabling acts. The root of the problem lay in the inability or unwillingness of local governments to use this power aggressively for purposes of protection. Some advocates of natural areas protection stressed "reform from below," but most reformers questioned whether working within the existing division of authority would reap substantial rewards. Most importantly, there was skepticism about the ability of local officials to transcend the parochialism imposed by dependence on the property tax as the major source of revenue. Even in cases of outright conflict with tangible community values, local governments traditionally demonstrated their preoccupation with expanding the property tax rolls. Given the intangible character of many of the values advocated by conservationists and environmentalists—natural diversity, scenic beauty—and the extralocal scope of many of the problems generated by development—water quality, outdoor recreational opportunities—the willingness of local officials to sacrifice revenue growth seemed quite problematical. As one report on natural areas protection noted:

. . .the decisions of local government are likely to reflect the system of values dictated by the profit and loss situation of the residents of that jurisdiction. The fact is that for reasons that are viewed as legitimate by residents, local jurisdictions will not—perhaps cannot—commit substantial land and water resources to the production of values realized by society at large.[20]

There also was serious doubt about the technical ability of local jurisdictions to identify the natural areas that required protection and to devise viable and effective regulations. As the report produced by Rockefeller Task Force on Land Use and Urban Growth noted:

19. There have been recent efforts to expand Corps authority over wetlands under Section 404 of the Federal Water Pollution Control Act Amendments of 1972 (P.L. 92-500). Under a ruling by the U.S. District Court for the District of Columbia in a suit brought by the National Wildlife Federation and the Natural Resources Defense Council, the Corps must regulate dredging and filling in all "waters of the United States" under guidelines established by EPA. NRDC v. Calloway, Civil Action No. 74-1242 (D.C. D.C., March 27, 1975). While the precise extent of expanded regulation is still not clear—the Corps has resisted a broad interpretation of "waters of the United States"—the Court order will significantly increase the federal role in natural areas protection.

20. U.S. Department of the Interior, Fish and Wildlife Service, National Estuary Study, Volume 1 (Washington, D.C., G.P.O., 1970), pp. 66-67.

Essential to the political and legal durability of any such ambitious scheme of protection is a first-rate planning process to assure that lands protected are carefully selected and truly merit protection and to make sure that reasonable development needs are planned for and met. At the local level, the difficulty of maintaining a high level of planning competence. . .increase(s).[21]

Finally, there was concern about the vulnerability of local regulations to legal challenge under the "takings clause" of the federal and state constitutions. Although the record varies from state to state, state courts for the most part have traditionally viewed restrictive regulations imposed by local jurisdictions with a skeptical eye. They have required compensation in many cases where the landowner was left without a clear marketable use for his property. Under these circumstances, regulation is merely a delaying tactic rather than a way of achieving conservation goals, because protection must ultimately be sought through acquisition. Of course, where a clear relationship to protection of public health and safety or other welfare goals could be demonstrated, local protective regulations have had more success in state courts. However, given the limited planning competence possessed by most local governments, it appeared doubtful that most local regulations for natural areas could be justified in that way.

In contrast to reliance on local government regulation, the exercise of direct authority by state government appeared to have a number of virtues. The states are not dependent on the property tax and are thus free of primary concern with land values. By the late sixties, furthermore, state governments were developing a sophisticated planning capacity in outdoor recreation and natural resource protection as a result of federal requirements and funding under the Land and Water Conservation Fund Act of 1965 and other functional programs.[22] Perhaps most importantly, many of the broad problems generated by rapid development in natural areas fell within traditional boundaries of state responsibility—water quality, fish and wildlife management, scientific research and education, and public safety standards. State governments could thus call upon existing agencies for guidance and coordination.

The states also enjoy a much better chance of avoiding legal difficulties in imposing restrictive regulations on a wide variety of privately owned natural areas, due to the existence of the public trust in navigable waters and submerged lands:

---

21. William K. Reilly (ed.), *The Use of Land: A Citizen's Policy Guide to Urban Growth* (New York, Thomas Y. Crowell, 1973), p. 121.

22. Richard Rubino and William Wagner, *The State's Role in Land Resource Management* (Lexington, Kentucky: Council of State Governments, 1972); Elizabeth Haskell, "New Directions in State Environmental Planning," 37 *Journal of the American Institute of Planners* 253 (1971).

The environmental proximity of public trust land to surrounding land held in absolute private ownership should however constitute another important factor in land use regulation under the public power. Regulations imposed on land closely connected with trust land will more likely be viewed as preventing a public harm rather than conferring a public benefit if such regulation is designed to protect rights recognized in trust lands.[23]

Finally, state regulatory programs incorporated the virtue of comprehensiveness. All of the natural areas within a large geographic area could be regulated by a single authority with a single set of standards and procedures. The vagaries of the local regulatory "lottery" could thus be avoided.

After 1965, proposals and recommendations for direct state-level regulation of a variety of natural areas thus began to appear with increasing frequency, effectively setting the agenda for state legislative discussion and action.

Wetlands

In 1965, Massachusetts and California became the first states to assert state powers over dredging and filling of wetlands. In Massachusetts, a Coastal Wetlands Act authorized the imposition of "protective orders" upon wetlands areas by the State Department of Natural Resources.[24] In California, the legislature authorized the formation of the San Francisco Bay Conservation and Development Commission, which was given authority to prohibit ecologically undesirable dredging and filling.[25] Both of these pioneering initiatives were responses to local conditions and the concerns of local interest groups, but they provided a major impetus to further advocacy and study of wetlands protection across the nation.

Perhaps of greatest importance were two federal studies. In 1966, Congress authorized the Interior Department to conduct a study of estuarine pollution. The next year, it also authorized a broader study of estuary use conflicts. Thanks to the Massachusetts and California initiatives and the

---

23. Mary Eikel and W. Scott Williams, "The Public Trust Doctrine and the California Coastline," 6 *The Urban Lawyer* 519 (1974), p. 562. For a detailed discussion of the "protection of existing public rights" doctrine, see Fred Bosselman, David Callies, and John Banta, *The Taking Issue* (Washington, D.C. Council on Environmental Quality, 1973).

24. The best general source on the origins and operation of the Massachusetts program is Fred Bosselman and David Callies, *The Quiet Revolution in Land Use Control* (Washington, D.C., G.P.O., 1971), pp. 205-234.

25. The Bay Commission was not given formal permitting authority over dredging and filling until after it completed the plan authorized by the original legislation of 1965. But the exercise of police power authority was clearly forecast in the initial statute. See E. Jack Schoop and John Hinten, "The San Francisco Bay Plan: Combining Policies With Police Power," 37 *Journal of the American Institute of Planners* 2 (1971).

substantial concern felt by several members of Congress, particularly Representatives John Dingell of Michigan and Herbert Lenzer of New York, a major concern of both studies was the improvement of regulatory and management processes for the protection of wetlands. The National Estuarine Pollution Study, issued in 1970, praised the Massachusetts legislation and encouraged its "adoption and adaptation" by other states.[26] The National Estuary study, also issued in 1970, declared that

Effective and adequately enforced zoning can regulate use of estuarine and Great Lakes lands and prevent unnecessary destructive dredging and filling of submerged and intertidal lands, as has been demonstrated in Massachusetts and in the San Franciso Bay area of California.[27]

Bosselman and Callies' *Quiet Revolution* also did a great deal to encourage legislative innovation on wetlands protection. Their book included extensive and favorable evaluations of what had happened in both states. With regard to Massachusetts, Bosselman and Callies found that

With more than two-thirds of coastal wetlands covered by protective orders, either recorded or pending, the consensus is that the coastal program has been a qualified success—qualified only by the considerable time required to issue the orders. Conservationists appear to be satisfied with the restrictions contained in coastal orders once adopted and with the fact that about half of the coastal wetlands in the state have now been protected, and that orders are or soon will be pending against most of the rest.[28]

The evaluation of the San Francisco program was even more positive:

To date, the Bay Commission has been remarkably successful. It has faced the powerful development interests and the traditionally sacred concepts of home rule and emerged with relatively few scars.[29]

As a result of these significant endorsements by federal agencies and a number of other well-publicized studies undertaken by such private organizations as the National Wildlife Federation and The Open Space Institute, the protection of wetlands through state-level regulation was firmly on legislative agendas by 1971.[30] While the wetlands issue has been somewhat overshadowed in recent years by concern with shorelands protection, it remains an active topic of debate and discussion in numerous legislatures.

---

26. U.S. Congress, *The National Estuarine Pollution Study,* op cit., pp. 399-400.

27. U.S. Department of the Interior, *National Estuary Study,* Volume 1, op. cit., p. 64.

28. Bosselman and Callies, *The Quiet Revolution,* op. cit., p. 225.

29. Ibid., p. 123.

30. Will Johns, *Estuaries—America's Most Vulnerable Frontiers* (Washington, D.C., National Wildlife Federation, 1969); Peter Johnson, *Wetlands Preservation* (New York, Open Space Institute, 1969).

Shorelands

The need for state-level regulation of land use in shoreland areas reached national prominence primarily through the efforts of two closely related federal groups, the National Council on Marine Resources and Engineering Development and the Commission on Marine Science, Engineering and Resources, both established by Congress in 1966.[31] Taking their cue from pioneering action by Wisconsin and California, both agencies responded to manifestations of concern by scientists, conservationists, and environmentalists by stressing state-level reform of land use control in shoreland areas.

In 1967, the Marine Council formed an Inter-Agency Task Force on Multiple Use of the Coastal Zone. A major national conference convened by this task force in 1968 brought together more than 100 state and federal officials to discuss the urgent need for rearrangement of land use authority in the coastal zone. This meeting played a central role in alerting state officials to the emerging federal concern with reform of coastal shorelands planning and control and familiarizing them with the concept of reclaiming some degree of authority over land use from local government.[32] Perhaps of even greater ultimate significance was the final report of the Commission on Marine Science, Engineering and Resources (the Stratton Commission), issued in January 1969. One of the primary conclusions of the Stratton Commission was the need for state-level responsibility:

After reviewing the various alternatives, the Commission finds that the States must be the focus for responsibility and action in the coastal zone. The State is the central link joining the many participants, but in most cases, the States now lack adequate machinery for that task. An agency of the State is needed with sufficient planning and regulatory authority to manage coastal areas effectively and to resolve problems of competing uses. Such agencies should be strong enough to deal with the host of overlapping and often competing jurisdictions of the various Federal agencies. Finally, strong State organization is essential to surmount special local interests, to assist local agencies in solving common problems and to effect strong interstate cooperation.[33]

---

31. On the origin of these two agencies, see Edward Wenk, *The Politics of the Ocean* (Seattle, Washington, University of Washington Press, 1972).

32. National Council on Marine Resources and Engineering Development, *Report on the Seminar on Multiple Use of the Coastal Zone* (Washington, The Council, November, 1968). See also Harold F. Wise and Associates, *Intergovernmental Relations and the National Interest in the Coastal Zone of the United States* (Washington, D.C., G.P.O., March 1969). Both of these documents are currently available from NTIS.

33. Commission on Marine Sciences, Engineering, and Resources, *Our Nation and the Sea: A Plan for National Action* (Washington, D.C., G.P.O., January 1969), pp. 56-57. For a more detailed discussion of the Commission's reasoning, see also *Panel Reports, Volume I: Science and Environment* (Washington, D.C., G.P.O., January 1969), Part III.

The importance of this recommendation was magnified by the fact that the Nixon administration incorporated the concept of state-level responsibility in proposed national legislation establishing federal grants for coastal zone management activities.[34] Although the proposed legislation dictated no specific intergovernmental formula, it was clear that direct exercise of the police power by state government, based upon a competent planning process, was at the heart of the proposal. With passage of the Coastal Zone Management Act (P.L. 92-583) in 1972, the issue of expanding state authority over shorelands attained widespread recognition. Indeed, as one of the few environmental spending programs to come out of the Nixon years, coastal zone management has been accorded extraordinary attention among state legislators and executive officials. Due to the particular structure of the federal program, which encourages the states to engage in a study and planning phase before undertaking legislative action, passage of the act did not immediately precipitate widespread statutory reform. But as the study and planning phase ends in 1976 for some states, and 1977 for the rest, state legislative agendas will soon be crowded with proposals for reallocation of authority over the shorelands.

Critical Environmental Areas

The need for broad state planning and regulation of environmentally sensitive areas was first argued prominently in 1969-70 drafts of the ALI's Model Code. Based upon the work of ecologists and planners and the concerns of conservationists and environmental organizations, the critical areas section of the Code envisioned state-level involvement in the control of development in at least two types of areas: those with some unique or unusual ecological value, and those which posed some particularly dangerous natural hazard. The language dealing with unique natural areas was an elaboration and endorsement of earlier state experimentation with wetlands regulation (Massachusetts, California), shorelands protection (Wisconsin), and designation of conservation areas (Hawaii). The inclusion of natural hazards was conceived and justified as a logical extension of traditional state responsibility for protecting public health and safety.

Like the Stratton Commission report, the ALI Model Code was significant both in itself and as the basis for proposed federal legislation. It is well-known that the Code directly set the stage for the Florida Land and Water Management Act of 1972, the first statute to authorize state protection of critical environmental areas. It is perhaps less well-known that the Code

---

34. The background of the Administration proposal is discussed in detail by Wenk, *The Politics of the Ocean,* op. cit., Chapter 3. The initial Administration bill was S. 3183 (91st Congress), introduced in January 1970.

was also the prime source for the national land use legislation proposed by the Nixon administration in 1971. It was this suggested legislation and the subsequent congressional hearings (which continued through 1975) that placed the issue of critical areas protection on state legislative agendas. In clear contrast to the traditional acquisition strategy, the Administration proposal forthrightly and unambiguously endorsed the need for states to exercise their police power authority over a variety of natural areas. This concept, while challenged, has been maintained in all subsequent drafts of the legislation. Over the past few years, this approach has been endorsed by a number of other influential organizations, such as the Council of State Governments.

WETLANDS PROTECTION LEGISLATION

Table IV-1 presents the basic data on the diffusion of wetlands protection legislation. The typical innovative statute incorporates two aspects of reform:

1. It establishes a set of explicit policy criteria and/or a planning process for the identification and protection of ecologically significant private wetlands.

2. It vests in a state agency the authority to enforce these protective criteria or planning principles through a review and permit process.

As with the other innovative legislation examined in this study, no specific formula of intergovernmental relations is held to be an essential component of the innovation. Beyond the common denominator of active state responsibility, there are wide differences from statute to statute in allocation of authority between state and local government.

There is a very striking pattern of regional variation evident in Table IV-1. Of the fourteen states that adopted wetlands protection legislation as of December 1975, nine were in the Northeast. Of the remaining five, four are in the South. Wetlands protection legislation is clearly an Atlantic Seaboard phenomenon, with strongest emphasis in the Northeast. Only Michigan, with passage of inland wetlands legislation in 1972, has broken the pattern of regional concentration.

Within the Northeast, the order of adoptions was what might be expected from previous research. The initial state to enact a statute was Massachusetts (1965), traditionally a leader in New England and the nation. The next two were Connecticut and Maine, which frequently look to Massachusetts for legislative leadership. With enactment by a major mid-Atlantic state in 1970 (New Jersey), diffusion of the legislation to the other states of the Northeast was speeded.

TABLE IV-1

DIFFUSION OF WETLANDS PROTECTION LEGISLATION
(As of December 1975)

State	Year of Adoption	Statute
Massachusetts	1965, 1968[1] * * *	Ann. Laws of Mass. Ch. 130 Section 105; Ch., 131 Section 40; 40A
Maine	1967 * *	Me. R.S.A. Title 38 Section 471 to 478
Connecticut	1969, 1972[1] * *	Conn. Gen. Stat. Section 22a-28 to 22a-35; 22a-36 to 22a-45
New Jersey	1970 * *	The Wetlands Act of 1970, N.J. S.A., Section 13.9A-1 to 13.9A-10 Md. C.A.,
Maryland	1970 * *	Natural Resources, Section 9-101 to 9-501
Georgia	1970 * *	Coastal Marshlands Protection Act of 1970, Code of Ga. Ann. Section 45-136 to 45-147
New Hampshire	1971 * *	N.H.R.S.A. Section 483A:1-A to 483A:6
North Carolina	1971 * *	N.C.G.S. Section 113-229; 113-230
Rhode Island	1971, 1974[1] * * *	General Laws R.I. Section 2-1-13 to 2-1-25
Michigan	1972 *	Wilderness and Natural Areas Act, Mich. Stat. Ann. Section 13-734(1) to 13-734(13)
Virginia	1972 * *	Virginia Code of 1950, Section 62.1-13.1
Delaware	1973 * * *	The Wetlands Act, Del. C.A. Section 7-6601 to 7-6620
Mississippi	1973 * *	Coastal Wetlands Protection Law, Miss. Code Ann. Section 49-27-1 to 49-27-69
New York	1973, 1975[1] * * *	Tidal Wetlands Act, McKinney's Consol. Laws of N.Y. BK. 17½, Section 25-0101 to 25-0601 Freshwater Wetlands Act, McKinney's Consol. Laws of N.Y., BK. 17½, Section 24-0101 to 24-1303

Proposed Legislation[2]

Wisconsin (Defeated by House, 1974) * *
Florida (Passed by House, Defeated by Senate, 1975) * * *

---

* Inland Wetlands Only
* * Coastal Wetlands Only
* * * Comprehensive—Inland Wetlands and Coastal Wetlands

1. Initial legislation amended.
2. Reported out favorably to a full chamber during the last two sessions.

The diffusion rate is somewhat more rapid than average for legislative innovations in the current era: fourteen states over a ten-year period. Adoptions were fairly evenly distributed from 1970 through 1973, with two or three enactments per year. In the last two years, however, the pace has slowed down markedly. No enactments were recorded in 1974, and only one in 1975. Only two legislative proposals reached both chambers for a vote in those years.

A number of factors seem to account for the decline of legislative activity.

First, the urgency of wetlands protection in inland states has not been firmly established. All the states which acted through December 1975 are coastal states. Except for Michigan, all have started with coastal wetlands protection. Inland wetlands protection has come only later, and not in all of the states.

This focus on coastal wetlands is easy to explain. The problems of land development in such areas are more obvious and dramatic, although not necessarily more ecologically significant, than the problems of development on inland wetlands. Most of the studies which set the agenda for legislative action were limited to the problems of coastal wetlands. As a result, inland wetlands protection has yet to be viewed as a high priority in many of the inland states.

Inland wetlands protection has also been bogged down by the opposition of agricultural interests, particularly in the Midwest. Farmers' opposition was a critical factor, for example, in the defeat of comprehensive wetlands legislation in Wisconsin in 1974 and 1974.

In southern coastal states which have not yet embraced the innovation, Florida, South Carolina, Louisiana, and Texas, wetlands protection remains highly controversial. In these states, unlike those of the Northeast, dredging and filling of private wetlands is a major economic activity. Developers and industrialists in these states have vigorously opposed wetlands protective legislation at the state level and were instrumental in the defeat of such legislation in the Florida Senate in 1975. Extensive professional endorsements, particularly by scientists, have not been sufficient to end the controversy.

Finally, there is the nagging matter of legal uncertainty over the constitutional validity of extremely restrictive regulation of wetlands. Some state courts have upheld state regulation, but others have not. As a result, the question of whether or not to compensate private owners of wetlands has become a confusing and divisive issue in state legislative debates, particularly in the South where traditional ideas about private property rights remain particularly strong.

SHORELANDS PROTECTION LEGISLATION

Dates of adoption of shorelands protection legislation are presented in Table IV-2. The typical innovative statute has two fundamental components:

1. It establishes a set of state policy criteria and/or a planning process for determining the appropriate use of land in a defined shoreland zone.

2. It provides for state regulatory control of development in the shoreland zone, in accordance with the policy criteria and/or plan.

In sharp contrast to wetlands protection legislation, the record on shorelands protection reveals little variation in regional receptivity. Adoptions have been distributed almost evenly across the regions—four in the Northeast, two in the South, three in the West, and four in the Midwest. Wisconsin originated shorelands protection legislation in 1966 and was followed by Minnesota and Michigan. The legislation spread to the Northeast and the West in the early seventies and has penetrated the South during the last two years. This wide dispersion of adoptions is, of course, evidence of strong national influences.

The overall rate of diffusion has been slightly faster than average, fourteen states in the nine years since first enactment. The pattern of legislative activity over time is irregular. Only three states adopted between 1966 and 1970; but in 1971, there was a burst of five enactments. In subsequent years, the rate of adoptions had again slowed, with only one in 1973 and 1974 and two in 1975. This relatively slow pace is likely to be only a preface, however, to a new surge of legislative activity once the planning phase of the federal coastal zone program ends.

The federal program is clearly the dominant influence on the diffusion of coastal shorelands legislation among the states. Under the Coastal Zone Management Act, federal funds are provided to those states willing to meet federal guidelines in planning and implementing state laws to protect the land along their coasts. As a result, state officials in all thirty ocean and Great Lakes coastal states are currently conducting studies and making plans prior to proposing shorelands protective legislation or amending existing laws. Twelve coastal states already have coastal shorelands legislation. Most, if not all, of the remaining eighteen states with coastal shorelands are likely to act once their planning periods end in 1976 and 1977. Except in Maine and California (which have both enacted statutes), proposals for state regulation of coastal shorelands have not been highly controversial. The concept enjoys extensive professional endorsement, and even local governments have supported such laws in many states—although they have typically attempted to limit the size of the shoreland zone to be placed under state jurisdiction.

71

TABLE IV-2

DIFFUSION OF SHORELANDS PROTECTION LEGISLATION
(As of December 1975)

State	Year of Adoption	Statute
Wisconsin	1966***	Wis. S.A., Section 59.971; 144.26
Minnesota	1969, 1973[1]**	M.S.A., Section 105.485, 105.49
Michigan	1970**	The Shorelands Protection and Management Act of 1970. Mich. Stat. Ann. Section 13.1831 to 13.1845
Rhode Island	1971**	General Laws of R.I. Section 46-23-1 to 46-23-16
Vermont	1971*	V.S.A. Title 10, Chapter 49, Section 1421 to 1426
Maine	1971, 1974[1]***	Me. R.S.A. Title 12, Section 4811 to 4814
Washington State	1971***	Shoreline Management Act of 1971, R.C.W.A., Section 90.58.010 to 90.58.930
Oregon	1971, 1973[1]**	O.R.S. Section 191.110 to 191.180; 215.010 to 215.190
Delaware	1972**	The Beach Preservation Act of 1972. Del. C.A. Section 6801 to 6809
California	1972**	California Coastal Zone Conservation Act, California Public Resources Code, Section 27000 to 27650
Alabama	1973**	Code of Alabama, Title 8, Section 312 to 320
North Carolina	1974**	Coastal Area Management Act of 1974, N.C.G.S. Section 113A-100 to 113A-129
Hawaii	1975**	H.R.S., Section 205A-1 to 205A-32
Montana	1975*	The Natural Streambed and Land Preservation Act of 1975, R.C. of Mont., Section 26-1509 to 26-1523

*Inland Shorelands Only
**Coastal Shorelands Only
***Comprehensive—Inland Shorelands and Coastal Shorelands

1. Initial legislation amended.

Beyond the good prospects for coastal shorelands legislation, inland shorelands are also widely recognized as needing protection from land development. Vermont, and more recently (1975) Montana, have enacted specific inland shorelands protection statutes. Maine has two laws, one for coastal shorelands and one for inland shorelands. The existing laws of Wisconsin and Washington state are comprehensive, covering both coastal and inland shorelands.

CRITICAL ENVIRONMENTAL AREAS PROTECTION LEGISLATION

The designation and regulation of critical environmental areas by state government is perhaps the most widely discussed and most controversial innovation in land use governance. Critical area statutes provide state agencies with a broad grant of discretionary authority over land use. Regulatory responsibility is not limited to a specific category of land (shoreland, wetland, etc.) but, at the prerogative of the agency, may be invoked to cover a wide variety of areas. In scope of coverage, then, critical areas statutes represent the most significant "recapture" of regulatory authority by state governments among all the natural areas statutes.

Table IV-3 presents the data on diffusion of critical environmental areas protection legislation. The typical statute has two basic components:

1. It establishes a set of state policy criteria and/or a planning process for the identification and designation of critical environmental areas on a statewide basis.

2. It provides a means for the state to exercise protective regulatory authority over development in the designated critical areas.

Florida initiated the innovation in 1972 with passage of the Land and Water Environmental Management Act, but its action has stimulated no further adoptions in the South. The most active region in embracing this innovation has been the West, where five states have enacted the legislation over three years. Two other western states came close to passing legislation in 1975, Idaho and Arizona. In Arizona, proposed legislation was defeated in the Senate at the last moment by only a few votes. The order of adoptions in the West more or less follows that which might be expected from previous analysis of legislative leadership in land use. Oregon and Nevada introduced the innovation to the region in 1973 and were followed by Colorado in 1974 and Wyoming in 1975. These states, along with California, also demonstrated the greatest receptivity to innovation in growth management within the western region. Outside the West, there have been

TABLE IV-3
DIFFUSION OF CRITICAL ENVIRONMENTAL
AREAS PROTECTION LEGISLATION
(As of December 1975)

State	Year of Adoption	Statute
Florida	1972	Florida Environmental Land and Water Management Act of 1972, Fla. Stats. Ann., Section 380.05
Nevada	1973	Nev. R.S., Section 321.640 to 321.810
Minnesota	1973	Critical Areas Act of 1973. M.S.A., Section 116G.01 to 116G.14
Oregon	1973	O.R.S., Section 215.010 to 215.990
Colorado	1974	C.R.S., Section 106-7-101 to 106-7-502
Maryland	1974	The Public Gen'l Laws of Md., Article 88C, Section 1-12
Wyoming	1975	The State Land Use Planning Act., Wyo. S.A., Section 9-849 to 9-862

Proposed Legislation[2]

Georgia (Defeated by House, 1974)
Wisconsin (Defeated by House, 1974)
Iowa (Passed by House, tabled in Senate, 1975)
Idaho (Defeated by House, 1975)
Arizona (Passed by House, defeated by Senate, 1975)
South Dakota (Passed by House, defeated by Senate, 1975)
New Hampshire (Defeated by House, 1975)

---

1. The Utah legislature passed a critical areas act during its 1974 session, but it was repealed by statewide referendum, November 1974.

2. Reported out favorably to a full chamber during last two sessions.

only scattered adoptions, Minnesota in the Midwest and Maine and Maryland in the Northeast. The most striking feature is the absence of any of the major industrial, urbanized states. With the exception of Florida, the innovative states are largely rural and agricultural, with small populations.

The rate of diffusion through 1975 was quite rapid, seven states over a span of four years. Following Florida's adoption in 1972, the pace of action increased markedly in 1973 (three adoptions) and 1974 (two adoptions).

However, as with wetlands and shorelands legislation, there was a slow-down in adoptions during 1975. Despite extensive legislative activity, only Wyoming enacted a critical environmental areas protection statute in 1975.

Several factors which impeded acceptance of the innovation were repeatedly emphasized in legislative debates during the past year.

One is that the adoption of wetlands and shorelands protection statutes has diminished the urgency of legislative action on critical environmental areas protection. Once wetlands or shorelands statutes, or both, are adopted, the need for general protection seems less pressing.

Another is the cost. Current economic considerations are discouraging state legislatures from setting up new and elaborate programs, particularly when the programs promise no significant economic improvements for citizens. With federal funds no longer in the offing as they were when the Jackson bill appeared likely to pass, advocates of natural areas protective legislation must now compete with advocates of other state-financed programs.

A third factor, which also affects wetlands and shorelands legislation, is the argument over compensation to owners of land which will be subject to severe restrictions on development. In Arizona, for instance, critical areas legislation was defeated in 1975 due to a dispute between House and Senate over a just compensation formula.

CONCLUSION

Each of the three types of state legislation discussed in this chapter—wetlands protection, shorelands protection, and critical environmental areas protection—demonstrates a different focus of diffusion. As Table IV-4 illustrates, wetlands statutes have been adopted primarily in the Northeast, with some spread into the coastal states of the South. Protection of critical environmental areas has been of greatest interest to legislators in the West. Protection of shorelands, on the other hand, has had substantial success in all four regions of the nation. With a strong push from the federal government, it seems to have transcended the "normal" region-by-region diffusion pattern.

Each of the three types of legislation had diffused at greater than average speed through December 1975. We have attributed this primarily to the strong efforts of the federal government in publicizing the issues and, in the case of shorelands, subsidizing the expenses of state-level programs. The above-average diffusion rate is also due to the nationwide efforts of the loose coalition of voluntary groups and organizations which constitute the "environmental movement." In 1975, however, the rate of

TABLE IV-4

SUMMARY STATISTICS:
DIFFUSION OF NATURAL AREAS
PROTECTION LEGISLATION

	TYPE OF LEGISLATION		
Adoption Information	Wetlands	Shorelands	Critical Environmental Areas
Date of First Adoption	1965	1966	1972
Total Number of Adoptions	14	14	7
Most Adoptions in One Year	3 (1971)	5 (1971)	3 (1973)
Adoptions by Region			
Northeast	9	4	1
South	4	2	1
Midwest	1	3	1
West	0	5	4

adoptions showed a marked decline from previous years. In the case of shorelands, this decrease is likely to be temporary, because many states are already committed to the consideration of innovative legislation. But with regard to wetlands and critical environmental areas, the decline in legislative activity seems likely to be long-standing unless there is a new upsurge of federal stimulation and voluntary group activity.

Table IV-5 shows the time interval, in years, between adoption by the first state (designated by 0) and adoption by other states. There are no outstanding national legislative leaders, but the table does reveal consistent regional leaders: Maine in the Northeast, North Carolina in the South, Minnesota in the Midwest, and Oregon in the West.

TABLE IV-5

SUMMARY STATISTICS: STATE ACTION ON NATURAL AREAS PROTECTION LEGISLATION
(Time Interval Since First Adoption, in Years)

State	Wetlands	Shorelands	Critical Environmental Areas
Alabama	—	8	—
Alaska	—	—	—
Arizona	—	—	—
Arkansas	—	—	—
California	—	7	—
Colorado	—	—	2
Connecticut	6	—	—
Delaware	10	8	—
Florida	—	—	0
Georgia	7	—	—
Hawaii	—	10	—
Idaho	—	—	—
Illinois	—	—	—
Indiana	—	—	—
Iowa	—	—	—
Kansas	—	—	—
Kentucky	—	—	—
Louisiana	—	—	—
Maine	4	6	—
Maryland	7	—	2
Massachusetts	0	—	—
Michigan	9	5	—
Minnesota	—	4	1
Mississippi	10	—	—
Missouri	—	—	—
Montana	—	10	—
Nebraska	—	—	—
Nevada	—	—	1
New Hampshire	8	—	—
New Jersey	7	—	—
New Mexico	—	—	—
New York	10	—	—
North Carolina	8	9	—
North Dakota	—	—	—
Ohio	—	—	—

(Continued)

TABLE IV-5 (Continued)

State	Wetlands	Shorelands	Critical Environmental Areas
Oklahoma	—	—	—
Oregon	—	6	1
Pennsylvania	—	—	—
Rhode Island	8	6	—
South Carolina	—	—	—
South Dakota	—	—	—
Tennessee	—	—	—
Texas	—	—	—
Utah	—	—	—
Vermont	—	6	—
Virginia	9	—	—
Washington	—	7	—
West Virginia	—	—	—
Wisconsin	—	0	—
Wyoming	—	—	3

V. CONCLUSIONS

Since 1971, when Bosselman and Callies completed *The Quiet Revolution in Land Use Control,* innovative statutes on land use have continued to spread among the states quite rapidly. Even during the recession years of 1974 and 1975, the momentum of legislative activity was maintained, and numerous adoptions were recorded. Clearly, the reassertion of state authority over the use of land is more than a passing fad or an aberration limited to a few states. However, as the preceding chapters have indicated, the three categories of reform and the nine specific statutes differ significantly in patterns of diffusion. This chapter summarizes these differences across the full range of categories and statutes, assesses the future prospects for diffusion in each category of innovation, and presents some personal conclusions about the need for further federal stimulation of state action.

PATTERNS OF DIFFUSION

Legislative Leadership

Perhaps the most striking finding about the diffusion of innovative land use statutes is that, contrary to the historical pattern documented by earlier studies, legislative leadership has not been consistently exercised by the more populous, affluent, urbanized, and industrialized states within each region. Only in the category of growth management, where California has led the West and Virginia and Florida have led the South, has the traditional pattern prevailed. In the other categories, most innovations have either been originated or embraced earliest within particular regions by smaller rural states which have usually lagged in receptiveness to innovation: Vermont and Maine; South Dakota and North Dakota; Montana, Hawaii, and Washington. In many of the larger states, land use innovations have not even reached the stage of serious legislative consideration, much less adoption.

In large part, this deviation from historical patterns can be explained in terms of a simple stimulus-response model. Since the late sixties, there has been a major shift in population growth patterns. Growth pressures are now focused in the peripheral, lightly populated states of the Southwest, Southeast, upper Midwest and upper New England rather than in the traditional urban heartland of the Northeast and Midwest. Indeed, states such as New York and Pennsylvania are actually beginning to lose population. Of course, the larger industrialized states still have significant growth problems, particularly in the still expanding suburban areas. But they are not of the same relative magnitude and urgency as those facing the smaller, rural states.

has lacked one or two elements of the crucial combination of circumstances specified above. The future prospects for each of these innovations will be considered in more detail below.

Diffusion Rates

With regard to the rates of diffusion, the statutes examined fall into three basic categories:

Below Average (Less than one adoption per year on average)	—	Mandatory Local Zoning Regulation, Large-Scale Industrial and Commercial Development Siting.
Above Average (Between one and two adoptions per year on average)	—	Mandatory Local Comprehensive Planning, Mandatory Local Subdivision Control, Wetlands Protection, Shorelands Protection, and Surface Mine Siting.
Far Above Average (Two or more adoptions per year on average)	—	Power Plant Siting and Critical Environmental Areas Protection.

In historical perspective, innovative land use statutes generally display a remarkably good record of acceptance. Projecting present trends, all but two statutes will easily best the average diffusion rate of twenty years/twenty states identified in previous studies.

Power plant siting seems well on its way to being one of the fastest diffused legislative initiatives in recent American history. For reasons discussed above, the innovation has been able to transcend the normal regional pattern. The question mark in this category is critical environmental areas legislation. The rapid diffusion during the past four years is based upon an extraordinary set of circumstances that will not prevail in the future—the prominence accorded the newly developed ALI Model Code, the publicity surrounding proposed national land use legislation, the anticipation of federal grants in aid under the national legislation, the vibrance and political clout of the environmental movement at the peak of its strength. The absence of these conditions clouds the prospects for maintenance of an extremely rapid diffusion rate.

PROSPECTS FOR FUTURE LEGISLATIVE ACTION

Growth Management

The best prospects within this category belong to mandatory comprehensive planning legislation. There has been a significant quickening of interest in this innovation during the past year in those areas facing the greatest growth pressures: the West, South, and upper Midwest. Washington and New Mexico, Iowa and Michigan, North Carolina and Tennessee seem likely to join their neighbors in embracing the innovation during the next few years. It is doubtful that the pace of six adoptions achieved in 1975 can be maintained, but two to three adoptions per year seems a reasonable estimate of the diffusion rate in the near future.

Although the innovation seems to be on the verge of breaking out of the normal region-by-region pattern into a more rapid nationwide diffusion process, there are still several influences that will continue to impede the spread of the statute. One factor is uncertainty over the future funding levels of the HUD 701 program. As one recent study of comprehensive planning across the nation concluded, "In every city we studied, the 701 program was either the primary source of ongoing financial support or a critical element in the original comprehensive planning effort. In this era of the New Federalism. . ., it is perplexing to watch while repeated efforts are made to eliminate the only local capacity-building program presently in operation."[1] Of course, the states can choose to cover the additional costs of mandatory comprehensive planning themselves, and several (Colorado, Wyoming, Oregon) have at least partially done so. However, the greater the direct cost of innovation to the states, the greater the reticence to embrace the statute.

A second factor impeding diffusion is serious professional disagreement over the wisdom of imposing plans upon unwilling local governments. As previously noted, the ALI Code rejects the concept of mandatory local planning with the argument that comprehensive plans produced merely because of legal requirements most likely will be bad plans. Another study suggests that "State mandated local planning is likely to be less effective than state supported local planning. Carrots and not sticks are needed to build local planning capacity."[2] Of course, there are many equally strong advocates of mandatory planning, but the point is that the lack of professional consensus provides ammunition to legislative opponents of the innovation, and impedes more rapid diffusion.

Prospects for the future diffusion of mandatory local subdivision control legislation are also favorable. Often incorporated in the same broad statute as mandatory local comprehensive planning, this innovation

---

1. Lawrence Susskind and Anne Aylward, "Comprehensive Planning: A State of the Art Review of Concepts, Methods, and the Problems of Building Local Capacity," Unpublished Paper Prepared for the Advisory Commission on Housing and Urban Growth; Cambridge, Mass. (August 25, 1975), p. 83.

2. Ibid., p. 81.

achieved a large number of adoptions in 1975 as well. However, to a larger extent than mandatory comprehensive planning, the innovation has been concentrated in a single region of the nation. Unless the innovation can break out into another region or regions, the future pace of diffusion will slow markedly as the remaining prospects in the West (Montana, Utah, and Washington) are exhausted. The most likely regions for future legislative action are the upper Midwest, where Iowa and Michigan have already indicated legislative interest, and the South, where Florida seems a probable candidate to join Virginia in adopting the innovation in the next year or two.

In a very direct manner, the progress of mandatory subdivision control is tied closely to the spread of mandatory local comprehensive planning. Many states already require all counties and municipalities with functioning planning commissions to enact subdivision control ordinances in accordance with state standards. As these states pass mandatory planning laws, the subdivision control innovation will follow naturally.

The only general factor impeding the diffusion of mandatory local subdivision control legislation is the fact that many states have passed a related innovation which diminishes the urgency of legislative action. These states have imposed a state-wide environmental review of certain aspects of subdivision platting applications—typically including water supply, sewage treatment, and grading-erosion standards. Examples of this approach are found in the laws of Maryland, Florida, Michigan, and Minnesota. This type of legislation does not eliminate the need for comprehensive subdivision control ordinances at the county and municipal levels, but it does lessen the incentive to require local action. To the extent that this approach spreads, the diffusion of mandatory local subdivision control legislation is likely to be slowed.

The innovation with poorest prospects in this category is mandatory local zoning regulation. The same factors which have caused this innovation to diffuse relatively slowly through 1975 will continue to impede future diffusion: professional discontent with the cumbersomeness, passivity, and negativism of zoning regulation; conservative ideological opposition to officially mapped restrictions upon the use of land; concern about the high cost of zoning administration; and diversion of attention to new techniques and methods of growth management. Just as the other two innovations in growth management, the diffusion of mandatory local zoning regulation has been concentrated so far in the West and the most likely adopters in the next few years are also in the West. Following the widely publicized example of Oregon, mandatory local zoning was strongly supported by the governor and many state legislators in Washington state in 1975. Although the legislation failed to win committee approval, the legislature is likely to consider the innovation again in 1976. In Montana, the planning law enacted in 1975 requires local governing bodies to classify land under their jurisdiction into six categories. These classifications are to be used as the basis for differential property tax assessment. The Montana legislature chose this approach because of the cost and unwieldiness of zoning, but the foundation for mandatory local zoning has been laid if the adopted alternative fails to control development effectively.

Outside the West, prospects for mandatory local zoning legislation are poor. In the Northeast, efforts to reform local zoning laws still are focused on the courts. In the South, zoning traditionally has had scant support. In the Midwest, there is some possibility of legislative action by states of the northern Great Plains; South Dakota, North Dakota, and Iowa. Nebraska has already become the only state outside the West to adopt the innovation. However, opposition by financially strapped local governments and by farmers—as exemplified in the Iowa legislative debate during 1975—promises to make the struggle for innovation very difficult in each of these states.

Siting

The innovation with the greatest promise of rapid diffusion during the next few years is surface mine siting. The nation is just entering a period of intense exploitation of surface coal, shale, and other energy-related materials. The issue of proper siting has reached a high peak of visibility from West Virginia to Montana. The environmental movement has embarked on a nationwide campaign to strengthen state surface mining laws, an effort which has reached its most prominent expression in proposed federal legislation which has twice passed Congress. The legislation is being considered again by the 94th Congress despite continuous Presidential vetoes.

Adoption of innovative surface mine siting laws so far has been focused in the northern Great Plains, with scattered adoptions in the South and West Coast. The most likely candidates for adoption in the near future are the neighboring states of the Great Plains—Minnesota, Wyoming, Nebraska, and Colorado. Minnesota, for example, was one of the first states to vest its state regulatory agency with the authority to designate certain lands unsuitable for surface mining on the basis of nonreclaimability. Adding broader land use considerations is a significant but incremental addition to existing law. Another region likely to enjoy considerable legislative activity during the next few years is the South. Recent statutes in South Carolina and North Carolina, for example, provide state regulatory agencies with considerable discretion to deny surface mining permits on a number of environmental grounds, including preservation of fish and wildlife. This incipient recognition of land use conflicts is likely to be translated into an explicit legislative mandate as surface mining pressures increase in these states.

The major imponderable in surface mine siting is adoption by the major coal-producing states of the Appalachian region—Pennsylvania, Ohio, Kentucky, and West Virginia. These states have such a major investment in the surface mining of coal that any significant slowdown presents a serious threat to jobs. Thus, receptiveness will depend heavily upon how the siting issue is addressed in their legislatures. If approached completely from the environmental preservation perspective—i.e., adding an additional layer of state land use controls to existing regulations—it is doubtful that the innovation will achieve much success in these states. The coal industry is simply too powerful, too well-connected, and too economically vital. If, however, the innovation is approached from a more positive perspective, such as that envisioned in the proposed national bill, the chances of rapid diffusion are brighter. The recent California statute provides an example of the positive approach to surface mine siting. In addition to imposing regulatory controls at the state level, it obligates the state agency to engage in an advance planning process through which mineral resource areas of "statewide or national significance" can be identified. The state agency also is authorized to preempt local development controls if it finds that local decisions will impede exploitation of such designated resource areas. The difficulty with the positive planning approach, of course, is that it is much more expensive and technically challenging than the simple permitting process which most states have authorized. Thus, even if the opposition of coal operators can be at least partially deflected, the California-type surface mine siting statute may run into the same type of budgetary constraints than have been impeding the diffusion of other innovative land use statutes.

Prospects for future diffusion are also good for power plant and transmission line siting, although it is doubtful that the extremely rapid pace of the early 1970s can be maintained. The basic problem remains—insuring an adequate supply of electric power while protecting environmental and community values—but the siting issue has decreased in urgency as the nation's consumption of electricity has declined since 1974. Some states still face immediate challenges—Montana, Arizona, New Mexico, California—but in many others, utilities have shelved plans for further expansion in the near future. Indeed, most of the states facing significant problems have already passed legislation, leaving future diffusion in the hands of states without an urgent reason to act.

On the other hand, power plant siting legislation has already diffused so widely across the nation that it has almost achieved the status of a legislative norm, a standard program which all states are assumed to have. In addition, the continuing interest of the federal government has been demonstrated by the Ford administration's proposed Energy Independence Act (H.R. 2650) which would vest the Federal Energy Administration with power plant siting authority if the states failed to act within a specified period of time. These factors will insure that the issue of power plant siting remains on the legislative agenda in states that have not yet adopted the innovation.

The likely candidates for legislative action during the next several years are in the South—North Carolina, Texas, Georgia—and the Northeast—Pennsylvania and New Jersey. The rate of diffusion is likely to be at least two adoptions per year.

The poorest prospects in this category of legislation are for the most comprehensive statute—large-scale commercial and industrial development siting. The intensive publicity accorded the Maine, Vermont, and Florida experiences, as well as the proposed national land use legislation, have put the issue on many legislative agendas; but only a few states have adopted the innovation. The primary reason is quite explicit in legislative debates: During a recession, legislators are not interested in further undermining the likelihood of industrial and commerical expansion by adding an additional layer of state development controls. Of course, the effects of the recession are temporary and may not substantially impede diffusion a few years from now. However, there are also more long-lasting impediments to adoption. Foremost among these is the growing skepticism about according wide discretion to government agencies for planning and permitting purposes. There was a strong element of this distrust in the defeat of the New Hampshire and Utah legislation during 1975 as well as the legislative rejection of Vermont's land use plan. Second, statewide site planning and control costs a considerable amount of money. Third, in a number of states, the urgency of state-level action is diminished by the existence of quite sophisticated local industrial development and siting authorities. Most of the states that have embraced the innovation acted in response to the lack of *any* local controls, rather than out of a general conviction that existing local controls should be supplemented or preempted.

The most likely candidates for adoption in the near future are in the West—Utah, Montana, and Idaho—and the upper Midwest—Iowa and North Dakota. It is unlikely that there will be much legislative activity in the Northeast, the prior focus of diffusion. An average of one adoption per year is the probable rate of diffusion during the forseeable future. In the absence of a major federal initiative, this statute will be one of the slowest diffusing innovations.

Natural Areas Protection

Shorelands protection legislation is likely to be the most rapidly diffusing type of statute in this category during the next few years. Having completed the planning and study phase under the national coastal zone management program, a number of coastal states are ready to introduce innovative statutes for legislative action in 1976 and 1977 sessions. The regions of greatest activity will be the South—where South Carolina, Georgia, and Texas are excellent prospects—and the Northeast—where New York, Pennsylvania, and Massachusetts are likely candidates for adoption.

Prospects also seem good for inland shorelands legislation. As the intensity of recreational development beside lakes and ponds increases, there is increasing recognition of the need for state guidance and supervision of local controls. During the next few years, the focus of legislative activity is likely to be in the Great Plains states of the upper Midwest and West—Wyoming, North Dakota, South Dakota, Minnesota—where lake-oriented recreation is a growing industry. Legislative consideration of inland shorelands protection is also likely in New England.

Critical environmental areas legislation has diffused very rapidly through 1976, but the prospects for further diffusion are more guarded. The major blow to the future prospects of this legislation was the failure of the national land use legislation. In the absence of anticipated federal funding, state legislatures have viewed the innovation much more skeptically, particularly because critical areas regulation may easily result in court-imposed compensation costs. Prospects are also clouded by the growing ideological discontent with "big government" and broad grants of discretion to administrators and planners. However, this is not to say that the critical environmental areas legislation will sink into obscurity. Some legislative activity will continue in the next few years in the West and upper Midwest. The governors of Idaho, Montana, and Washington have strongly supported such legislation in the recent past. Arizona almost passed a statute in 1975, and in New Mexico, the state Land Use Advisory Council is likely to recommend protective legislation in 1976.

In the upper Midwest, where Minnesota has already enacted a statute, the issue also continues to be actively debated. The governor of Michigan has made critical environmental areas protection part of his legislative program, although a proposed statute has yet to be reported out of committee.

The Wisconsin legislature considered, but failed to adopt, a bill in 1974. Proposed legislation passed the House but not the Senate in both Iowa and South Dakota in 1975. It will be reconsidered in both states in the next sessions of the legislatures.

The most likely course of diffusion during the next few years is that adoptions will slow from the extraordinary rate of 1972 through 1976 to an above-average pace of one or two enactments per year. Should a national land use initiative supporting the identification and regulation of critical environmental areas be resurrected, the diffusion rate would again increase.

The poorest prospects in this category belong to wetlands protection legislation. Most coastal wetlands are covered already by existing protection programs under wetlands statutes or broader shorelands statutes. The remaining coastal states without protection programs are mostly in the South, where dredging and filling assumes the greatest economic importance and the "taking issue" constitutes a major impediment to more assertive state action. Among the southern states, Florida seems the most likely candidate for adoption of a wetlands protection statute in the near future; but as the 1975 defeat demonstrated, it will be a difficult political struggle.

Most of the legislative action on wetlands protection during the next few years will involve extension of existing coastal wetlands statutes to cover inland wetlands. Massachusetts, Connecticut, Rhode Island, and most recently (1975) New York, have enacted this broader-type coverage, and the other states of New England and the Northeast seem likely to follow.

Prospects for future diffusion of independent inland wetlands protection legislation are very limited. Michigan is still the only state which has enacted a freestanding inland wetlands statute. Legislative interest among other inland states has been nonexistent. It will require a major agenda-setting effort on the part of an environmental organization and/or the federal government to stimulate further action.

IMPLICATIONS FOR FEDERAL POLICY

Throughout this study, the central role of the federal government in stimulating state innovation on land use governance has been emphasized. Federal action has assisted the diffusion of state land use legislation in two ways: (a) by setting the agenda for legislative action by the states through reports, conferences, proposed legislation, and so forth, and (b) by providing funds for innovative efforts through existing federal programs or new legislative enactments. The agenda-setting role has already been accomplished effectively for most of the innovative statutes considered in this study. With the possible exception of surface mine siting, the innovations are well-publicized and widely discussed, due largely to federal efforts. The federal role in providing financial and technical assistance is, however, subject to doubt. During the last two years, a number of initiatives designed to assist the diffusion of innovative state statutes have been stymied in Congress or the Executive branch. The absence of this anticipated federal aid will severely retard the progress of several types of legislation.

A critical re-examination of the rationale for federal financial aid and federal program standards is now taking place. Why should the federal government encourage the states to adopt certain types of land use legislation? Under what circumstances are uniform state programs and national coverage desirable? The strongest case for stimulative federal action can be made in regard to three statutes: surface mine siting, critical environmental areas protection, and shorelands protection.

In response to the Arab oil embargo, the nation has recognized that it is dependent on the production of coal. A large and growing proportion of coal production comes from surface mines. There is a direct and vital national interest in facilitating the identification and the exploitation of surface coal reserves while mitigating the enormous environmental impact surface mining produces. Although the basic innovation promises to diffuse rapidly even in the absence of proposed national legislation (H.25, 94th Congress), a federal grant-in-aid program which would stimulate diffusion seems vital on two grounds: (a) in the absence of federal funds, many states are likely to forego the more expensive advance planning component that is vital to meaningful reconciliation of environmental and economic interests; and (b) given the direct national dependence on coal, there is a need for nationwide standards to guide state decisionmaking on surface mine siting.

The argument for a federal aid program for state critical environmental areas protection also rests upon the perception of a direct national interest. Major natural areas such as the Florida Keys, the Columbia Gorge, the Outer Banks of North Carolina, and others of this type that might be identified and protected under state programs are of more than statewide significance. Such areas, which exist in every state, are recreational, scenic, and ecological assets of national importance. They are used by citizens of all the states; they support unique species of flora and fauna; and they contribute significantly to the overall diversity and beauty of the United States. Because these areas are too large and too expensive to be purchased by

90

any level of government, there is a strong and compelling case for federal action to encourage the states to use their police power authority.[3]

Finally, there is a direct national stake in coastal shorelands protection. A federal grant-in-aid program is, of course, already underway in this area. In the preamble to the National Coastal Zone Management Act of 1972, Congress explicitly recognized that there are a number of vital and tangible national interests at issue in coastal shorelands regulation, including recreation, navigation, fisheries, energy development, and military security. Although the original bill does not include substantive standards to which state programs must conform, there recently have been efforts to stimulate a more direct assertion of the national interest in coastal protection. Through 1976, the coastal zone management program remains the only federal aid program which stimulates and facilitates state action on reform of land use governance.

Three or four years ago, a similarly strong case could have been made with regard to the direct national interest in power plant siting. The nation faced critical power shortages, and few states were equipped to deal with continued siting conflicts. Today, the situation has changed dramatically. Electric power consumption is down by 5 percent since 1974, and many utilities have shelved future expansion plans. Almost half the states have siting programs to resolve conflicts and limit delays, including the states which are the focus of current power production plans. Given the interconnection of electric systems and the development of new generating technologies, power can be generated almost anywhere in the country and transmitted where it is needed. The urgency of insuring that each state solve its own siting problems is thus diminished, as long as the bulk national supply is adequate. Of course, many serious problems still plague the states— in particular, the siting of nuclear plants. If, for example, proposed initiatives on nuclear siting should be passed in Colorado and Oregon in 1976, the federal government may have to invervene and set nationwide standards

---

3. It is doubtful whether the proposed national land use legislation sponsored by Senator Jackson and Representative Udall was the appropriate vehicle for federal encouragement of state innovation on critical environmental areas protection. The critical areas component of those proposals was intermixed with a wide variety of other planning and regulatory requirements that diminished the strength of the federal stimulus. In addition, there was much confusion about the issue of including national policy standards to guide the states in identifying and regulating critical environmental areas. The ultimate resolution, in response to opponents' charges of "federal zoning," was to omit any substantive nationwide standards. This omission seriously weakened the importance and impact of the proposed legislation. In short, there remains a need for federal action on critical environmental area protection, but in the form of more focused and policy-oriented legislation. See Lyday, op. cit.

for the location of nuclear generating stations. In general, however, the power plant siting problem does not seem to require federal action such as that proposed by the Ford administration (H.R. 2650, 94th Congress). The prospects for continued diffusion are good, even in the absence of federal legislation.

Another area where the context has changed during the past five years is wetlands protection. A large number of states have already passed wetlands programs, and protection of coastal wetlands in states without explicit statutes is incorporated and supported in the federal coastal zone management program. Thus, protection of inland wetlands in non-coastal states and some coastal states is left. It is far from clear that there is a direct and compelling national interest in the protection of these wetlands. Although some inland wetlands have demonstrable interstate significance as aquifer recharge areas and wildlife spawning grounds, the preservation of most of these areas for conservation, recreation, or aesthetic purposes is basically a matter of concern to individual states. Thus, a program of financial support for state programs devoted to inland wetland protection does not seem warranted.

The siting of large-scale commercial and industrial developments was included as a matter of federal interest and concern in the proposed Jackson-Udall legislation. However, beyond a general liberal belief that planned development is better than unplanned development, the rationale for direct federal support of state programs is extremely weak. Certainly, there is a national interest in clean air and water; but national air and water pollution standards for major developments are already established under existing EPA programs. It is difficult to comprehend why the federal government should go beyond these criteria to subsidize state-level programs for controlling the rate and location of development. The need for state-level siting control in those states where local land use controls do not exist or where they are unreasonably restrictive or permissive is evident. But this is clearly a state-by-state determination, and not a matter the federal government should push strongly. In the absence of a strong federal initiative, the innovation will continue to diffuse quite slowly. But this deliberateness is perhaps as it should be, given the complexity and cost of broad-gauged state siting control.

Finally, with regard to mandatory local planning, subdivision control, and zoning, there is no basis for direct federal encouragement and support of diffusion. The HUD 701 program indirectly facilitates the passage of innovative statutes by defraying costs that would otherwise fall on local and state governments. The national land use legislation also would have stimulated indirectly the diffusion of these statutes by providing funds for state technical assistance to localities. The reduction of funds in the 701 program and the defeat of anticipated funding from the Jackson bill undoubtedly have impeded faster diffusion of the three mandatory local growth management statutes; but it is hardly a federal responsibility if state governments are unwilling to spend their own money on important local functions. Indeed, federal money for expanded planning, zoning, and subdivision control capacities remains available under general revenue sharing and community development block grants if local governments choose to spend it on these purposes. In short, the federal role in reform of the basic planning and zoning enabling statutes ought to remain limited to advice and agenda-setting, as in the 1920s. The coverage of controls differs so widely among the states, and the state-local relationship is so sensitive that stronger federal support for these innovations seems inappropriate and unnecessary.